Advent, Christmas and Epiphany
in the Domestic Church

Advent, Christmas and Epiphany in the Domestic Church

CATHERINE AND PETER FOURNIER

IGNATIUS PRESS   SAN FRANCISCO

"Got the Saints and Apostles backing up from behind."

*For the lessons from Madonna House, the McPhees, and all the other
Nazareth friends, the priests who have become part of the family
(especially the Sicilian), and generations of faithful parents.*

*A special thanks to six wonderful, patient children:
Faustina, Andrew, Sarah, Matthew, Jonathon, and Robert.
You taught us everything we know.*

Scripture quotations are from the Holy Bible, Revised Standard
Version, Catholic Edition. Old Testament © 1952; Apocrypha © 1957;
Catholic Edition, incorporating the Apocrypha, © 1966; New Testament
© 1946; Catholic Edition © 1965, by the Division of Christian Education
of the National Council of the Churches of Christ in the United States
of America. All rights reserved.

Book design by Peter and Catherine Fournier.

Copyright © 2001 by Domestic Church Communications Ltd.,
Peter W. A. Fournier and Catherine A. Fournier.
All rights reserved.

Published by Ignatius Press, San Francisco.

ISBN 0–89870–859–1
Library of Congress Control Number 2001088852

Printed in the United States of America ∞

Contents

which have been accomplished among us, just as they were delivered to us by those who from the beginning were eyewitnesses and ministers of the word, it seemed good to me also,

Christmas in a Barn

It may sound strange, but some year we want to sleep in a barn on Christmas Eve. After Christmas Eve Mass, we would all drive to a friend's farm and sleep in their hayloft, above the cows and sheep. We would leave the presents, decorations and fancy clothes at home and experience for ourselves the birthplace of Jesus. Unfortunately, and I can't imagine why, the children have never been as impressed with this idea as we are. They yell, "No, No, No!" whenever we try to discuss it. Well, yes, we would miss the Christmas Eve feast at the grandparents, and, yes, there would be no tree with presents in the morning. We could live without that for one year, couldn't we?

"No, NO, NO!"

Our Christmas celebrations once followed the familiar pattern. A wreath on the front door, Christmas tree in the living room, school concerts and parties, and a two-day frenzy of driving through snowstorms, present-opening and feasting. Christmas Eve with in-laws, Christmas morning at home, Christmas Mass, then Christmas dinner with my parents, back to the in-laws on Boxing Day (the day after Christmas). On Christmas Eve we would force ourselves to stay awake until our hyped-up kids had gone to sleep so that we could bring out the Santa Claus gifts and fill the stockings. We would hope (usually in vain) for enough sleep to cope with the mother-and-adult-daughters-in-the-kitchen-making-a-turkey-dinner scene the next day. On Christmas morning it was hard to slow down enough to pay close attention at Christmas Mass, to thank God for the gift of His Son.

We were together as a family in body, but that is about all. Christmas time always felt a bit sad. We could tell we were missing something, though we had no idea what. Then Peter and I began praying regularly and saying evening prayers with the children. We found that regular prayer is like flying in a small airplane. You begin to see things from a different perspective. Familiar objects suddenly have a different orientation.

And from that vantage point, we saw the discrepancy between the observance of Christmas and the distortion of "Xmas". We realized that by trying to live both, we were contradicting ourselves and teaching our children that the values of the world are as important as the values of faith and eternity. We had to change.

But children are the original conservatives. Change makes them high-strung and irrational, prone to wild conclusions and persecution complexes. We decided the best way to ensure success (and avoid mutiny) was to change gradually, one thing at a time. Every year, we replaced an old tradition with a new one, preferably an activity that the children could participate in. And without any idea of where we were going, we set out to make our Christmas more devout and family-centered.

As a beginning, we built a Jesse tree. Peter and I were surprised by the effect of this simple activity. Every year, it brings a new perspective to Advent and Christmas. The next year, we replaced Santa Claus with Saint Nicholas and began to shift the focus of the season from gifts to joyful celebration (though gifts are still nice!). Next, we introduced an Advent wreath.

We have gained far more than we gave up. (Isn't that always the way?) By stripping away Santa Claus and Jingle Bells, by escorting Xmas out of our house and welcoming Christmas in, by praying together and working together, we have learned that the best Christmas was the first Christmas with a baby born to poor young parents in a barn. They had no decorated tree, no feast, no presents to give each other, not even a bed for the Baby. But in their poverty and simplicity, they welcomed the Light of Christ and gave Christmas to the world.

This book shares what we have learned. These are the ideas that have worked with our family and for others. We have included some favorite family activities, some crafts for you and the older children, some coloring pictures for the little ones, and profiled the most popular saints of the season. In addition, we have noted the numbers of relevant passages in the *Catechism of the Catholic Church* like this: (CCC 222). I encourage you to try some ideas—but not all at once!—and develop your own traditions. See what happens in your own domestic church.

And the chorus of "No, No, No!" gets quieter every year.

Family Activities

which you have been informed. In the days of Herod, king of Judea, there was a priest named Zechariah, of the division

before God, walking in all the commandments and ordinances of the Lord blameless. But they had no child, because Elizabeth was barren, and both were advanced in years. Now

The Advent Wreath

Every season of Advent is a new reminder of the promise of eternity (CCC 1020–29). Thus, Advent wreaths are made of evergreens to symbolize God's "everlastingness" and our immortality. (Purple is the liturgical color for Advent; green in the wreath symbolizes hope and new life.) Four candles—three purple or violet, which represent penance, sorrow and longing expectation, and one rose or pink, which represents the hope and coming joy—are used to represent the four weeks of Advent.

The custom of the Advent wreath originated in Germanic Europe. Wreaths were an ancient symbol of victory. In Christian symbolism, they represent the "fulfillment of time" in the coming of Christ and the glory of His birth. Wreaths of all kinds are round as a reminder of God's eternity and mercy.

Our family has an Advent wreath. We place our Advent wreath on our dinner table every evening through the season of Advent. We eat by its light alone. In the December darkness, the Light of God is brighter by contrast. The first week, the single candle seems very feeble and lonely. It reminds us of the faithful all over the world who are living in isolation or hostility. The second week, there are two lights, and we remember that Christ said, "Where there are two or more of you gathered in my Name, there also shall I be." The third week, we light the pink candle. We know Christmas is closer, and we think about the three members of the Holy Family. Finally, in the fourth week, all four candles are lit. We can see by their light to read the Nativity narratives from our Bible.

On Christmas Day, we replace the pink and purple candles with white ones. Our Advent wreath stays on the table for the twelve days between Christmas and Epiphany. Now, the candles symbolize our joy at the coming of Christ and our prayers of thanksgiving to God.

Making an Advent Wreath

Advent wreaths can be simple or elaborate, made from fresh material or from artificial greenery. It is important to use something green, which symbolizes the new life brought to us by the birth of Jesus, and that the wreath be circular as a reminder of eternity.

A fresh wreath requires:

- shallow bowl or dish
- oasis (also known as florist's foam, it is available from any florist)
- three purple candles
- one pink candle
- four white candles
- pine or cedar boughs, or ivy

Make the wreath by first soaking the oasis in warm water until it is completely saturated. Fit it into the bowl, carving it and packing it in tightly so that it will not shift around.

Then, carve four holes in the oasis for the candles. Place the candles in the holes you have made and begin sticking greenery into the oasis to cover it completely. It's nice to have some greenery trailing over the edges of the bowl and closely packed around the candles to hide all the foam.

If you keep the foam well watered, and don't let the candles burn down so low that they scorch the greenery, the wreath will last from the first Sunday of Advent until Epiphany.

A more permanent wreath requires:

- a plate or tray
- a four-candle candelabra or four small candlesticks
- three purple candles
- one pink candle
- four white candles
- artificial garland, holly branches, branches from an artificial tree, or some other artificial greenery

To make the wreath, arrange the candlesticks or candelabra on the tray. The tray allows the wreath to be moved easily. Then place the greenery around the candles in a pleasant arrangement. It can be embellished with red berries, a small creche, ribbons or whatever else is available.

Bless your wreath on the first Sunday of Advent by sprinkling it with holy water and saying a short prayer (Dads, this is your part!). In our home, we repeat the blessing each Sunday.

In some traditions, on the first Sunday of Advent, children write their Christmas letter to the Christ Child, Christkindl, who, accompanied by His angels, will bring the Christmas tree and all the good things on it and under it.

Another custom sees the secret exchange of names on the first Sunday of Advent. For the rest of the Advent season, small good deeds are performed for the "secret friend".

In Denmark, the Christmas season begins on December 1, with the lighting of a calendar candle. The candle is marked with twenty-four lines, one for each day before Christmas. The burning of the candle represents the waiting and preparing for Christ's coming.

Advent Wreath Prayers

While lighting the Advent wreath every evening through Advent, it seems appropriate to say a short prayer or blessing expressing some of the feelings this small ceremony invokes. The creatively challenged among us (my husband and I included) find this intimidating, to say the least. Prayers like the following offer some help in this area.

Week 1

Let us pray. Stir up Your might, we beg You, O Lord, and come, so that we may escape through Your protection and be saved by Your help from the dangers that threaten us because of our sins. You live and reign for ever and ever. Amen.

Week 2

Let us pray. O Father, stir up our hearts that we may prepare for Your only begotten Son, that through His coming, we may be made worthy to serve You with pure souls. We ask this through Christ our Lord. Amen.

Week 3

Let us pray. We humbly beg You, O Lord, to listen to our prayers; and by the grace of Your coming bring light into our darkened minds. You live and reign for ever and ever. Amen.

Week 4

Let us pray. Stir up Your might, we pray You, O Lord, and come; rescue us through Your great strength so that salvation, which has been hindered by our sins, may be hastened by the grace of Your gentle mercy. You live and reign for ever and ever. Amen.

The Jesse Tree

The Jesse tree is a symbol of Jesus' family tree. It also takes us through that first long Advent, which lasted from the Fall to the Incarnation. (CCC 117, 410–12, 461, 1095.)

After one of our children has lighted the Advent wreath and we have sung an Advent song ("O Come, O Come, Emmanuel" is our favorite), another child hangs the symbol for that day on the Jesse tree. Then Dad or one of the children reads the Bible passage, and we ask questions and talk about the reading.

When we added the Jesse tree reading to our evening prayer routine, Peter and I were surprised by the effect of such a simple change. As Advent goes on, the genealogical story gets closer and closer to Christmas morning and the birth of Jesus. It's exciting. The evening readings put a new perspective on Advent and Christmas for the family. We begin to realize that Jesus, Mary and Joseph were real people with histories and ancestors, just like us.

As the children get older they take turns with the readings. Often, they don't think the suggested reading is long enough. Especially the story of Joseph and the coat of many colors, "We can't just leave him there! We have to read on and find out what happens next!" So we do, and travel to Egypt and experience the famine with Joseph's brothers and laugh when they are all reunited. Finally, we reach the end of Advent. The weeks of preparation and waiting have helped us get ready for the wonder of Christmas Eve and Christmas Day.

Making the Jesse Tree

The symbols can be made out of cardboard, wood or cloth with the image drawn, painted or embroidered on it. Images cut from old Christmas cards and holy cards would be suitable as well. Each reading can be written on the back and an image representing the story on the front (an ark, an apple and a snake or a raven, for example). Because our symbols kept losing themselves, I made a wall hanging to keep them organized. It has four rows of pockets in the shape of candles, one for each symbol—for the four weeks of Advent.

The Jesse tree itself looks like this illustration; it can be made of wood dowels drilled and glued, rough sticks lashed together, wire, a banner wall hanging or even a large poster.

Advent, Christmas and Epiphany in the Domestic Church: Family Activities   www.Domestic-Church.com

Jesse Tree Symbols—First Week of Advent

First Monday of Advent
Genesis 1:24–28

First Sunday of Advent
1 Samuel 16:1–13

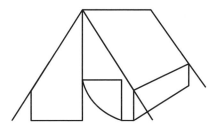

First Thursday of Advent
Genesis 12:1–7; 13:2–18

First Friday of Advent
Genesis 22:1–14

First Tuesday of Advent
Genesis 3:1–24

First Wednesday of Advent
Genesis 6:11–22; 8:6–12

First Saturday of Advent
Genesis 27:41—28:22

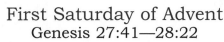

Jesse Tree Symbols—Second Week of Advent

Second Monday of Advent
Genesis 37:1–36

Second Sunday of Advent
Isaiah 9:2–7

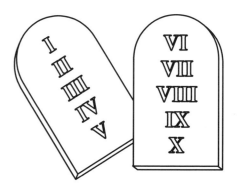

Second Tuesday of Advent
Exodus 20:1–17

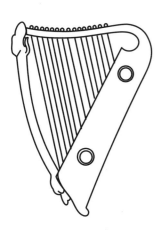

Second Friday of Advent
1 Samuel 16:14–23

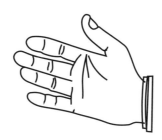

Second Wednesday of Advent
Numbers 6:22–27

Second Thursday of Advent
1 Samuel 3:1–21

Second Saturday of Advent
Psalm 23

Jesse Tree Symbols—Third Week of Advent

Third Monday of Advent
1 Kings 17:1–16

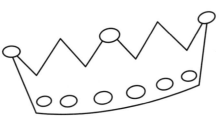

Third Sunday of Advent
1 Kings 3:3–28

Third Thursday of Advent
Jeremiah 31:31–34

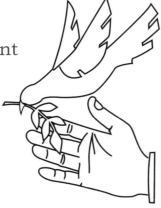

Third Tuesday of Advent
2 Kings 5:1–27

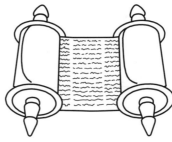

Third Wednesday of Advent
Isaiah 6:1–8

Third Friday of Advent
Nehemiah 13:10–22

Third Saturday of Advent
Hebrews 1:1–14

Jesse Tree Symbols—Fourth Week of Advent

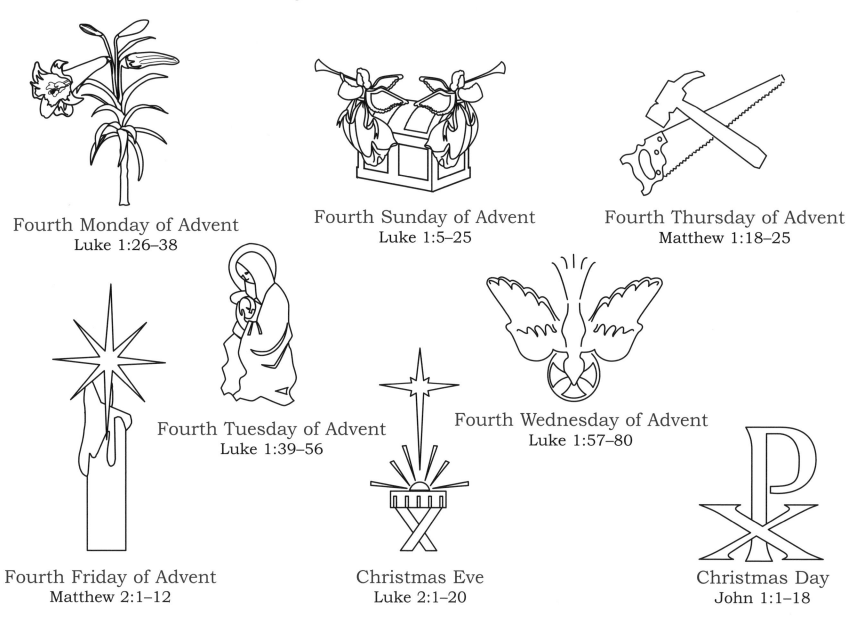

Fourth Monday of Advent
Luke 1:26–38

Fourth Sunday of Advent
Luke 1:5–25

Fourth Thursday of Advent
Matthew 1:18–25

Fourth Tuesday of Advent
Luke 1:39–56

Fourth Wednesday of Advent
Luke 1:57–80

Fourth Friday of Advent
Matthew 2:1–12

Christmas Eve
Luke 2:1–20

Christmas Day
John 1:1–18

Advent, Christmas and Epiphany in the Domestic Church: Family Activities   www.Domestic-Church.com

The "O" Antiphons

The "O" Antiphons, all beginning with the vocative "O", are sung or said from December 17 through 23, on the seven days before the Vigil of the Nativity. (CCC 1095–96, 2090.) The Antiphons are a collection of phrases from Biblical texts, singing of man's desire and longing for God. This longing, which has existed throughout the history of God's people from the beginning of time through Abraham, Moses and David, was fulfilled on the night when Emmanuel (God with us) was born.

The structure of the Antiphons makes them perfect for a family tradition. Some families draw the symbols of the Antiphons on circles of cardboard, felt, fabric or paper and hang them from ribbons on a banner or poster. The circles are turned to the wall, and as or after the Antiphon is sung or said, the circle is flipped to show the images. On Christmas Eve, all the images are visible.

December 17

O Wisdom, You came forth from the mouth of the Most High and reaching from beginning to end, You ordered all things mightily and sweetly. Come and teach us the way of prudence!

December 18

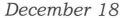

O Lord and Ruler of the house of Israel, You appeared to Moses in the burning bush and on Mount Sinai gave him Your Law. Come and with outstretched arm redeem us!

December 19

O Root of Jesse, You stand for an ensign of mankind; before You kings shall keep silence, and to You all nations shall have recourse. Come, save us and do not delay!

December 20

O Key of David, and Scepter of the House of Israel, You open and no man closes; You close and no man opens. Come and deliver him from the chains of prison who sits in darkness and in the shadow of death!

December 21

O Rising Dawn, Radiance of the Light eternal and Sun of Justice; come and enlighten those who sit in darkness and in the shadow of death!

December 22

O King of Nations and Desired of All, You are the cornerstone that binds two into one. Come, and save poor man whom You fashioned out of clay!

December 23

O Emmanuel, God with us, our King and Lawgiver, the Expected of nations and their Savior; come and save us, O Lord our God!

and the disobedient to the wisdom of the just, to make ready for the Lord a people prepared." And Zechariah said to the angel, "How shall I know this? For I am an old man,

Nativity Figures and the Christmas Crèche

Almost as common and popular as the Christmas tree, the Christmas crèche has an old and interesting history. Today, the Nativity scene helps us visualize, identify and meditate on the mystery and miracle of the Incarnation and the Nativity. (CCC 461, 525–28.) Adults and children alike are drawn to these scenes.

The Christmas crèche was originally assembled by Saint Francis of Assisi in 1293 in the woods of Greccio near Assisi, on Christmas Eve. He asked a man living in Greccio—a very holy person himself who was good friends with Saint Francis—for help in creating a scene in memory of the Infant, born at Bethlehem and bedded in a manger between a donkey and an ox. Saint Francis believed that this enactment of Christmas night would inspire the faith and devotion of the people of the region. He was right, and this tradition has continued and grown ever since.

Soon there were Christmas crèches in churches and homes. Moravian Germans brought the custom to the United States. Though Saint Francis first assembled what we know as the Christmas crèche, the oldest known picture of a "Nativity scene" dates from about 380. It is a wall decoration in a Christian family's burial chamber, discovered in 1877 in the Roman catacombs of Saint Sebastian.

Most families have a Christmas crèche, set in an honored position on the family altar or the mantle of the living room. Not just another decoration, a Christmas crèche in a Catholic home is a seasonal devotional object, a visual and tangible expression of faith. Family prayers can take place in front of the crèche, and it can become the center of the family's Advent preparations, as small acts of charity fill the manger with straw or written petitions are slipped underneath it.

Many crèches made of plaster, ceramic or wood are fragile. They are placed out of reach, so that the children see but don't touch and possibly damage the pieces. Understandable as this is, removing the crèche from the children's reach deprives them of the opportunity to learn.

Children learn through touching, exploring and playing, so why not give them a crèche they *can* play with?

Making "Playable" Cloth Nativity Figures

Materials

- Various fabric scraps such as:
  —blue and white for Our Lady
  —white for Infant
  —shades of brown for Joseph
  —flesh color for faces and hands, whatever "flesh" color you prefer
  —bright, rich colors for Wise Men
  —drab, rough textured fabric for Shepherds
  —warm, soft flannelette or cotton to use as swaddling clothes
- piece of lace or gold braid for Infant, approximately 10 cm (4 in.)
- bright or gold embroidered braid and trim for Wise Men
- darker, more somber trim for Joseph
- Lace for Mary's veil, if you wish
- bright buttons or small trinkets for the Wise Men's gifts
- embroidery floss: blue, brown, red, yellow or gold
- polyester fiberfill
- 1 cup of clean sand or small pebbles (look for these in pet or aquarium supply stores)
- some straw or yellow yarn
- wood or pipe cleaner for Joseph's staff

Equipment

- sewing scissors
- needle and thread or sewing machine
- pins
- embroidery needle

Sewing Terms

Baste —a temporary fastening, usually of long hand or machine stitches.

Clip —small, short cuts in the seam allowance at right angles to the seam, to allow the fabric to move and fold along the seam line, usually done on a convex curve.

Notch —small triangular notches cut into the seam allowance, in the same manner as clipping, usually done on a concave curve.

Hem —the raw or unfinished edge of fabric, turned under and sewn to prevent ravelling and to give a neat appearance; can be done with small invisible stitches or through all layers with a machine seam.

Pin —to fasten temporarily with pins before stitching.

Seam —line of stitching holding two or more pieces of fabric together, usually ⅝ inch away from a cut edge.

Seam allowance —the fabric between the raw edge and the seam, traditionally ⅝ inch.

Selvage —the finished edge along the sides of fabric, formed by the machine that wove the fabric.

Trim —to cut away excess fabric that would otherwise make a seam too thick or bunchy.

Right side —the outside of the material, the side that will show when item is finished.

Wrong side —the inside of the fabric, the side that will not show when item is finished.

Directions

Read instructions through carefully before beginning this project.

Note: Use 6 mm (¼ in.) seams throughout unless otherwise indicated.

Basic Adult Figure

1. Cut three body pieces, two bases, two head-dress pieces (front and back), two sleeves, two arms and one face piece.

2. Pin face piece to front body piece. Sew together around the edges. If it would be easier, you may embroider the face at this point.

3. Sew long sides of three body pieces together.

4. Create the face opening in the headdress by pinning a facing (cut an additional headdress piece of scrap fabric) to the headdress with the right sides together. Mark a desired face opening. Sew around the edges of this opening; cut out the opening, clip the seam and turn the facing to the inside. Press flat.

5. Fold and sew arm pieces into long tubes, closed at one end. Clip curves and turn right side out. Stuff firmly with polyester fiberfill.

6. Hem edge of sleeve (the wider edge) by turning under ⅛ inch and sewing. Apply trim if desired before sewing the sleeve together.

7. With right sides together, fold sleeves lengthwise and sew along the length, leaving the shoulder edge open.

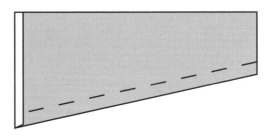

8. Turn right side out, and push one arm piece into each sleeve, adjusting to leave some "hand" showing. Pin arms into sleeves.

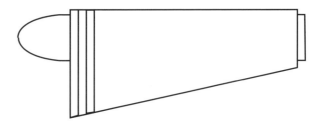

9. Depending on the size of figure and choice of headdress, you can attach the arms in one of two ways.

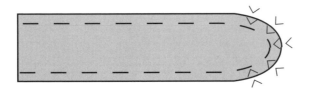

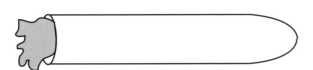

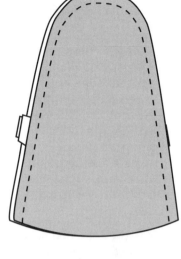

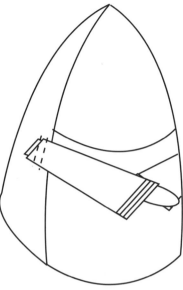

a. You can pin the sleeve and arm units to either side of the assembled body, arranging them at whatever angle pleases you. (Joseph could have one arm up to hold a staff; the Wise Men could have both arms forward to hold gifts; Mary might have her arms held out toward the Infant or at her sides.) By hand, or with your sewing machine, run a few seams across the end of the sleeves, making sure to catch the ends of the arms as well. This will be covered by the headdress.

Pin the headdress together and sew. Clip curves, and turn the headdress right side out.

10. Hem the bottom of the headdress, adding whatever trim or decoration you wish.
11. Baste or zig-zag the edges of two base pieces together.

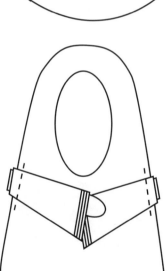

b. You can attach the sleeve arm units to the headdress by pinning them onto the long edges of the headdress pieces, again at a position and angle that pleases you. The simplest way to do this is to lay the front head piece in front of you, lay the sleeve arm pieces onto it pointing toward the center and each other, so that they will catch in the side seams, then lay the back piece, right side down, on top.

Pin the headdress together and sew. Clip curves, and turn the headdress right side out.

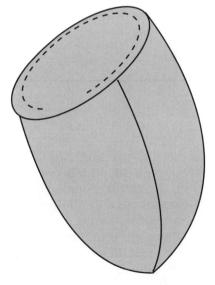

Turn the body inside out again and pin the base pieces to the bottom. Sew almost all the way around, leaving a few inches for stuffing. Turn it right side out again.

12. Stuff the body firmly with polyester fiberfill, ending with a few tablespoons of sand or pebbles. Turn under the remaining raw edges and hand stitch the opening. This can be a bit tricky, trying to keep the pebbles from falling out as you sew, but persevere; the weight helps the figures stand up.

13. You may choose to embroider the face at this point before the headdress is attached.

14. Pull the completed headdress over the completed body and tack it into place. You can hand sew all the way around the bottom edge and around the face, or you can anchor it with a piece of braid as a headband. This depends largely on the amount of handling you expect the figures to receive. Use more stitching for heavier use.

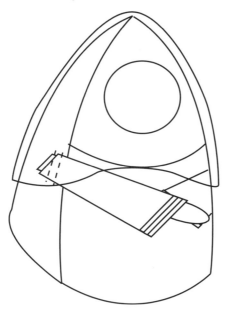

15. Arrange the arms in their desired positions; you may want to tack them in place as well. Sew a staff made from wood or pipe cleaner into Joseph's right hand. Attach the Wise Men's hands together so that they can hold their gifts.

16. If you haven't already done so, embroider the face as your final step. French knots for eyes, simple straight stitches or couching for eyebrows and mouths. Beards and mustaches can be made by sewing across the middle of short pieces of yarn or embroidery cotton, so that each end hangs free. Use several rows for a full beard, one or two pieces of yarn for a mustache. A considerable amount of personality can be added with the angle of the eyebrows and the placement of the eyes and mouth. Experiment.

Infant

1. Embroider facial features onto one piece.

2. Gather the piece of lace with a row of long stitches, pin it onto the raw edge around the top of your embroidered face as a halo, placing it so that it will be caught in seam.

3. Sew the front and back pieces together, right sides together, leaving an inch or so to stuff. Turn right side out, stuff and sew raw edges together.

4. Hem the swaddling clothes piece on all four sides. Wrap the Infant in it, like a shawl, so that it crosses in front. Tack the swaddling clothes in place.

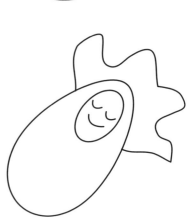

Manger

1. Cut one pattern piece from fabric, and, with right sides facing, fold the fabric in half lengthwise, as shown below. Stitch the raw edges together (leaving the ends open), and turn right side out.

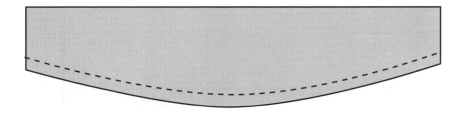

2. Stuff firmly. You will have a fat sausage shape that is fatter in the middle than it is at the ends. Bring the ends together to form a circle and stitch them together. This manger is more like a round pillow with a hole in the middle than the wooden crib shapes depicted on Christmas cards. The fatter middle sits a bit higher and props up the Infant's head, while the hole is just the right size to cradle the Infant's body.

3. Arrange straw along the top of the manger and place the Infant on top of the straw.

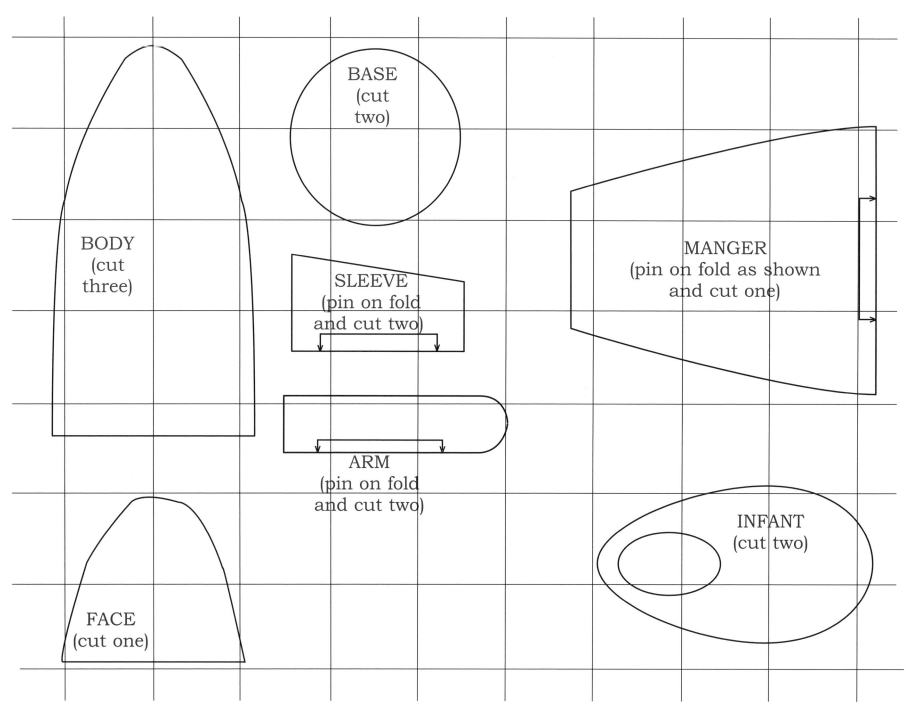

BASE
(cut two)

BODY
(cut three)

SLEEVE
(pin on fold
and cut two)

MANGER
(pin on fold as shown
and cut one)

ARM
(pin on fold
and cut two)

INFANT
(cut two)

FACE
(cut one)

Advent, Christmas and Epiphany in the Domestic Church: Family Activities

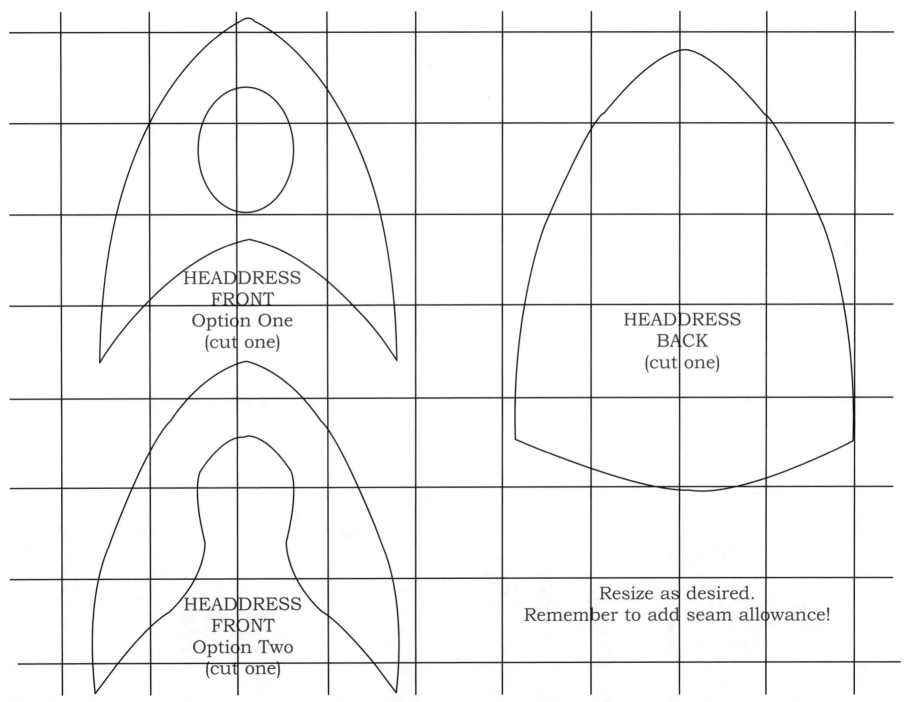

HEADDRESS
FRONT
Option One
(cut one)

HEADDRESS
FRONT
Option Two
(cut one)

HEADDRESS
BACK
(cut one)

Resize as desired.
Remember to add seam allowance!

Advent Hymns and Christmas Songs

During Advent we like to add the singing of Advent hymns to our evening prayers. Not only is song a wonderful way to pray (CCC 437, 461, 2655–58) but we have a lot of fun. (There is as much laughing and joking as there is singing!) Some of us are tone-deaf, while others can't remember lyrics at all. One year it took the whole of Advent to learn "O Come, O Come, Emmanuel" all the way through!

Sometimes it is difficult to find the words for Advent hymns and Christmas carols. (I can always remember the tune, but never the second verse.) Most collections of Christmas songs are all cluttered up with "Deck the Halls", "Jolly Old Saint Nicholas" and other secular songs. So, over the years, I have gathered a collection of true Christmas carols, all centered on the Nativity.

Here are some of my favorites.

Advent Hymns

O Come, Divine Messiah

O come, divine Messiah,
The world in silence waits the day,
When hope shall sing its triumph,
And sadness flee away.

> *Refrain*
> Sweet Savior, haste;
> Come, come to earth:
> Dispel the night and show thy face,
> And bid us hail the dawn of grace.

O thou, whom nations sighed for,
Whom priests and prophets long foretold,
Wilt break the captive fetters,
Redeem the long lost fold.

> *Refrain*
> Sweet Savior, haste;
> Come, come to earth:
> Dispel the night and show thy face,
> And bid us hail the dawn of grace.

Shalt come in peace and meekness,
And lowly will thy cradle be:
All clothed in human weakness,
Shall we thy Godhead see.

> *Refrain*
> Sweet Savior, haste;
> Come, come to earth:
> Dispel the night and show thy face,
> And bid us hail the dawn of grace.

Venez, Divin Messie

O Fils de Dieu, ne tardez pas;
Par votre corps donnez la joie,
À notre monde en désarroi.
Redites-nous encore,
De quel amour vous nous ignorent!
Venez, venez, venez!

> *Refrain*
> Venez, divin Messie,
> Nous rendre espoir et nous sauver!
> Vous êtes notre vie!
> Venez, venez, venez!

À Bethléem, les cieux chantaient,
Que le meilleur de vos bienfaits,
C'était le don de votre paix.
Le monde la dédaigne:
Partout les coeurs sont divisés!
Qu'arrive votre règne!
Venez, venez, venez!

> *Refrain*
> Venez, divin Messie,
> Nous rendre espoir et nous sauver!
> Vous êtes notre vie!
> Venez, venez, venez!

Vous êtes né pour les pécheurs.
Que votre grâce, O Dieu Sauveur,
Dissipe en nous la nuit, la peur!
Seigneur, que votre enfance,
Nous fasse vivre en la clarté.
Soyez la délivrance!
Venez, venez, venez!

The Angel Gabriel from Heaven Came

The angel Gabriel from Heaven came,
His wings as drifted snow, his eyes as
  flame:
"From God, all hail", the angel said to
  Mary,
"Mostly highly favored lady." Gloria!

"Fear not, for you shall bear a holy child,
By whom we shall to God be reconciled:
His name shall be Emmanuel, the long
  foretold:
Mostly highly favored lady." Gloria!

Then gentle Mary humbly bowed her
  head:
"To me be as it pleases God", she said,
"My soul shall praise and magnify his holy
  Name."
"Mostly highly favored lady." Gloria!

Of her Emmanuel, the Christ, was born
In Bethlehem, upon that Christmas morn,
And Christian folk throughout the world
  will ever say:
"Mostly highly favored lady." Gloria!

O Come, O Come, Emmanuel

O come, O come, Emmanuel,
And ransom captive Israel,
That mourns in lonely exile here,
Until the Son of God appear.
   Rejoice! Rejoice! Emmanuel,
   Shall come to thee, O Israel.

O come, thou Rod of Jesse, free
Thine own from Satan's tyranny.
From depths of hell Thy people save,
And give them vict'ry o'er the grave.
   Rejoice! Rejoice! Emmanuel,
   Shall come to thee, O Israel.

O come, O Dayspring, come and cheer
Our spirits by Thine advent here.
And drive away the shades of night,
And pierce the clouds and bring us light.
   Rejoice! Rejoice! Emmanuel,
   Shall come to thee, O Israel.

O come, Thou Key of David, come,
And open wide our Heavenly home.
Make safe the way that leads on high,
And close the path to misery.
   Rejoice! Rejoice! Emmanuel,
   Shall come to thee, O Israel.

O come, O come, Thou Lord of might,
Who to Thy tribes, on Sinai's height,
In ancient times did'st give the law,
In cloud and majesty and awe.
   Rejoice! Rejoice! Emmanuel,
   Shall come to thee, O Israel.

Another version

O come, O come, Emmanuel,
Redeem Thy captive Israel,
That into exile drear is gone,
Far from the face of God's dear Son.
   Rejoice! Rejoice! Emmanuel,
   Shall come to thee, O Israel.

O come, Thou Branch of Jesse! draw
The quarry from the lion's claw;
From the dread caverns of the grave,
From nether hell, Thy people save.
   Rejoice! Rejoice! Emmanuel,
   Shall come to thee, O Israel.

O come, O come, Thou Dayspring bright!
Pour on our souls Thy healing light;
Dispel the long night's lingering gloom,
And pierce the shadows of the tomb.
   Rejoice! Rejoice! Emmanuel,
   Shall come to thee, O Israel.

O come, Thou Lord of David's Key!
The royal door fling wide and free;
Safeguard for us the Heavenward road,
And bar the way to death's abode.
   Rejoice! Rejoice! Emmanuel,
   Shall come to thee, O Israel.

O come, O come, Adonai,
Who in Thy glorious majesty,
From that high mountain clothed with awe,
Gavest Thy folk the elder law.
   Rejoice! Rejoice! Emmanuel,
   Shall come to thee, O Israel.

will be impossible." And Mary said, "Behold, I am the handmaid of the Lord; let it be to me according to your word." And

Veni, Veni, Emmanuel

Veni, veni, Emmanuel,
Captivum solve Israel,
Qui gemit in exilio,
Privatus Dei Filio.
　　Gaude, gaude; Emmanuel,
　　Nascetur pro te, Israel.

Veni, O Jesse Virgula;
Ex hostis tuos ungula,
De specu tuos tartari,
Educ et antro barathri.
　　Gaude, gaude; Emmanuel,
　　Nascetur pro te, Israel.

Veni, veni, O Oriens;
Solare nos adveniens;
Noctis depelle nebulas,
Dirasque noctis tenebras.
　　Gaude, gaude; Emmanuel,
　　Nascetur pro te, Israel.

Veni, Clavis Davidica;
Regna reclude caelica;
Fac iter tutum supernum,
Et claude vias inferum.
　　Gaude, gaude; Emmanuel,
　　Nascetur pro te, Israel.

Veni, veni, Adonai,
Qui populo in Sinai,
Legem dedisti vertice,
In majestate gloriae.
　　Gaude, gaude; Emmanuel,
　　Nascetur pro te, Israel.

Christmas Hymns

Angels We Have Heard on High

Angels we have heard on high,
Sweetly singing o'er the plains.
And the mountains in reply,
Echoing their joyous strains.

　Refrain
　Gloria, in excelsis Deo!
　Gloria, in excelsis Deo!

Shepherds, why this jubilee?
Why your joyous strain prolong?
Say what may the tidings be
Which inspire your heav'nly song?

　Refrain
　Gloria, in excelsis Deo!
　Gloria, in excelsis Deo!

Come to Bethlehem and see,
Him whose birth the angels sing.
Come adore on bended knee
Christ the Lord, the newborn King.

　Refrain
　Gloria, in excelsis Deo!
　Gloria, in excelsis Deo!

See Him in a manger laid,
Whom the choirs of angels praise.
Mary, Joseph, lend your aid,
While our hearts in love we raise.

　Refrain
　Gloria, in excelsis Deo!
　Gloria, in excelsis Deo!

Sainte Nuit

Ô nuit de paix! Sainte nuit!
Dans le ciel l'astre luit;
Dans les champs tout repose en paix.
Mais soudain, dans l'air pur et frais,
Le brillant choeur des anges,
Aux bergers apparaît.

Ô nuit de foi! Sainte nuit!
Les bergers sont instruits;
Confiants dans la voix des cieux,
Ils s'en vont adorer leur Dieu;
Et Jésus en échange,
Leur sourit radieux.

Ô nuit d'amour! Sainte nuit!
Dans l'étable, aucun bruit;
Sur la paille est couché l'Enfant,
Que la Vierge endort en chantant:
Il repose en ses langes,
Son Jésus ravissant.

Ô nuit d'espoir! Sainte nuit!
L'espérance a relui:
Le Sauveur de la terre est né;
C'est à nous que Dieu l'a donné.
Célébrons ses louanges:
Gloire au Verbe incarné!

O Holy Night

O holy night! The stars are brightly
  shining,
It is the night of the dear Savior's birth!
Long lay the world in sin and error pining,
Till He appear'd and the soul felt its
  worth.
A thrill of hope, the weary world rejoices,
For yonder breaks a new and glorious
  morn!

Refrain
Fall on your knees,
Oh, hear the angel voices!
O night divine,
O night when Christ was born.
O night divine, O night divine.

Led by the light of Faith serenely beaming
With glowing hearts by His cradle we
  stand.
So led by light of a star sweetly gleaming,
Here come the wise men from Orient land.
The King of Kings lay thus in lowly
  manger,
In all our trials born to be our friend.

Refrain
Fall on your knees,
Oh, hear the angel voices!
O night divine,
O night when Christ was born.
O night divine, O night divine.

Truly He taught us to love one another,
His law is love and His gospel is peace.
Chains shall He break for the slave is our
  brother,
And in His name all oppression shall
  cease,
Sweet hymns of joy in grateful chorus
  raise we,
Let all within us praise His holy name.

Refrain
Fall on your knees,
Oh, hear the angel voices!
O night divine,
O night when Christ was born.
O night divine, O night divine.

Silent Night

Silent night, holy night!
All is calm, all is bright.
'Round yon Virgin, Mother and Child.
Holy Infant so tender and mild,
Sleep in Heavenly peace,
Sleep in Heavenly peace.

Silent night, holy night!
Shepherds quake at the sight.
Glories stream from Heaven afar,
Heav'nly hosts sing Alleluia,
Christ the Savior is born!
Christ the Savior is born.

Silent night, holy night!
Son of God, love's pure light.
Radiant beams from Thy holy face,
With the dawn of redeeming grace,
Jesus Lord, at Thy birth.
Jesus Lord, at Thy birth.

"Blessed are you among women, and blessed is the fruit of your womb! And why is this granted me, that the mother of

The Huron Carol

T'was in the moon of winter-time,
When all the birds had fled,
That mighty Gitchi Manitou,
Sent angel choirs instead;
Before their light the stars grew dim,
And wandering hunter heard the hymn:

Refrain
Jesus, your King is born,
Jesus is born,
In excelsis gloria.

Within a lodge of broken bark,
The tender Babe was found.
A ragged robe of rabbit skin,
Enwrapp'd His beauty round;
But as the hunter braves drew nigh,
The angel song rang loud and high.

Refrain
Jesus, your King is born,
Jesus is born,
In excelsis gloria.

O children of the forest free,
O sons of Manitou,
The Holy Child of earth and Heaven,
Is born today for you.
Come kneel before the radiant Boy,
Who brings you beauty, peace and joy.

Refrain
Jesus, your King is born,
Jesus is born,
In excelsis gloria.

O Come, All Ye Faithful

O come, all ye faithful,
Joyful and triumphant,
O come ye, O come ye to Bethlehem.
Come and behold Him,
Born the King of Angels!

Refrain
O come, let us adore Him,
O come, let us adore Him,
O come, let us adore Him,
Christ the Lord.

Sing choirs of angels,
Sing in exhultation.
Sing all ye citizens of heav'n above;
"Glory to God, glory in the highest!"

Refrain
O come, let us adore Him,
O come, let us adore Him,
O come, let us adore Him,
Christ the Lord.

Yea, Lord, we greet Thee,
Born this happy morning;
Jesus, to Thee be the glory giv'n;
Word of the Father,
Now in the flesh appearing,

Refrain
O come, let us adore Him,
O come, let us adore Him,
O come, let us adore Him,
Christ the Lord.

What Child Is This?

What child is this, Who, laid to rest,
On Mary's lap is sleeping?
Whom angels greet with anthems sweet,
While shepherds watch are keeping?

Refrain
This, this is Christ the King,
Whom shepherds guard and angels sing:
Haste, haste to bring Him laud,
The Babe, the Son of Mary!

Why lies he in such mean estate,
Where ox and ass are feeding?
Good Christian, fear: for sinners here,
The silent Word is pleading.

Refrain
This, this is Christ the King,
Whom shepherds guard and angels sing:
Haste, haste to bring Him laud,
The Babe, the Son of Mary!

So bring Him incense, gold, and myrrh,
Come peasant king to own Him,
The King of Kings, salvation brings,
Let loving hearts enthrone Him.

Refrain
This, this is Christ the King,
Whom shepherds guard and angels sing:
Haste, haste to bring Him laud,
The Babe, the Son of Mary!

Raise, raise the song on high,
The Virgin sings her lullaby:
Joy, joy, for Christ is born,
The Babe, the Son of Mary!

Once in Royal David's City

Once in royal David's city,
Stood a lowly cattle shed,
Where a mother laid her baby,
In a manger for His bed.
    Mary was that mother mild,
    Jesus Christ her little child.

He came down to earth from Heaven,
Who is God and Lord of all,
And His shelter was a stable,
And His cradle was a stall.
    With the poor, and mean, and lowly,
    Lived on earth our Savior holy.

And our eyes at last shall see Him,
Through His own redeeming love.
For that child so dear and gentle,
Is our Lord in heav'n above.
    And He leads His children on,
    To the place where He is gone.

Mary Had a Baby

Mary had a baby, O Lord,
Mary had a baby, O my Lord,
Mary had a baby, O Lord,
People keep a-comin' an' the train done
    gone.

What did she name Him? O Lord,
What did she name Him? O my Lord,
What did she name Him? O Lord,
People keep a-comin' an' the train done
    gone.

She named Him Jesus, O Lord,
She named Him Jesus, O my Lord,
She named Him Jesus, O Lord,
People keep a-comin' an' the train done
    gone.

Now where was He born? O Lord,
Where was He born? O my Lord,
Where was He born? O Lord,
People keep a-comin' an' the train done
    gone.

Born in a stable, O Lord,
Born in a stable, O my Lord,
Born in a stable, O Lord,
People keep a-comin' an' the train done
    gone.

And where did she lay Him? O Lord,
Where did she lay Him? O my Lord,
Where did she lay Him? O Lord,
People keep a-comin' an' the train done
    gone.

She laid Him in a manger, O Lord,
Laid Him in a manger, O my Lord,
Laid Him in a manger, O Lord,
People keep a-comin' an' the train done
    gone.

Mary had a baby, O Lord,
Mary had a baby, O my Lord,
Mary had a baby, O Lord,
People keep a-comin' an' the train done
    gone.

strength with his arm, he has scattered the proud in the imagination of their hearts, he has put down the mighty from

O Little Town of Bethlehem

O little town of Bethlehem,
How still we see thee lie,
Above thy deep and dreamless sleep
The silent stars go by.
Yet in thy dark streets shineth,
The everlasting light,
The hopes and fears of all the years
Are met in thee tonight.

For Christ is born of Mary,
And gathered all above,
While mortals sleep the angels keep
Their watch of wondering love.
O morning stars together,
Proclaim the holy birth,
And praises sing to God the King,
And peace to men on earth.

How silently, how silently,
The wondrous gift is given.
So God imparts to human hearts,
The blessings of His Heaven.
No ear may hear His coming,
But in this world of sin,
Where meek souls receive Him still,
The dear Christ enters in.

O holy Child of Bethlehem,
Descend to us we pray.
Cast out our sin and enter in,
Be born in us today.
We hear the Christmas angels,
The great glad tidings tell,
O come to us, abide with us,
Our Lord Emmanuel!

Hark! the Herald Angels Sing

Hark! the herald angels sing,
"Glory to the new-born King;
Peace on earth, and mercy mild,
God and sinners reconciled":
Joyful all ye nations rise,
Join the triumph of the skies,
With th'angelic host proclaim,
"Christ is born in Bethlehem."

Refrain
Hark! the herald Angels sing,
"Glory to the new-born King."

Christ, by highest Heaven adored,
Christ the everlasting Lord:
Late in time behold Him come,
Off-spring of the Virgin's womb!
Veiled in flesh, the Godhead see,
Hail th'incarnate Deity!
Pleased, as Man, with men to dwell,
Jesus, our Emmanuel!

Refrain
Hark! the herald Angels sing
"Glory to the new-born King."

Hail, the heav'n born Prince of Peace,
Hail, the Sun of Righteousness!
Light and life to all He brings,
Risen with healing in His wings.
Mild He lays His glory by,
Born that man no more may die;
Born to raise the sons of earth;
Born to give them second birth.

Refrain
Hark! the herald Angels sing
"Glory to the new-born King."

Come, Desire of nations, come,
Fix in us Thy humble home;
O, to all Thyself impart,
Formed in each believing heart!
Hark! the herald angels sing,
"Glory to the new-born King;
Peace on earth, and mercy mild,
God and sinners reconciled!"

Refrain
Hark! the herald Angels sing
"Glory to the new-born King."

We Three Kings of Orient Are

We three Kings of Orient are;
Bearing gifts we traverse afar,
Field and fountain, moor and mountain,
Following yonder star.

Refrain
O star of wonder, star of night,
Star with royal beauty bright,
Westward leading, still proceeding,
Guide us to thy perfect light.

Born a King on Bethlehem's plain,
Gold I bring to crown him again,
King forever,
Ceasing never,
Over us all to reign.

Refrain
O star of wonder, star of night,
Star with royal beauty bright,
Westward leading, still proceeding,
Guide us to thy perfect light.

Frankincense to offer have I;
Incense owns a Deity nigh;
Prayer and praising, all men raising,
Worship Him God most high.

Refrain
O star of wonder, star of night,
Star with royal beauty bright,
Westward leading, still proceeding,
Guide us to thy perfect light.

Myrrh is mine; its bitter perfume,
Breathes a life of gathering gloom;
Sorrowing, sighing, bleeding, dying,
Sealed in the stone-cold tomb.

Refrain
O star of wonder, star of night,
Star with royal beauty bright,
Westward leading, still proceeding,
Guide us to thy perfect light.

Glorious now behold Him arise,
King and God and Sacrifice.
Alleluia, Alleluia,
Earth to Heaven replies.

Refrain
O star of wonder, star of night,
Star with royal beauty bright,
Westward leading, still proceeding,
Guide us to thy perfect light.

Carol of the Bells

Hark to the bells, Hark to the bells,
Telling us all,
Jesus is King.

Strongly they chime, Sound with a rhyme
Christmas is here!
Welcome the King.

Hark to the bells, Hark to the bells,
This is the day,
Day of the King.

Away in a Manger

Away in a manger, no crib for a bed,
The little Lord Jesus laid down his sweet
head;
The stars in the sky looked down where
he lay,
The little Lord Jesus, asleep on the hay.

The cattle are lowing, the Baby awakes,
But little Lord Jesus, no crying he makes;
I love thee, Lord Jesus! look down from
the sky,
And stay by my cradle till morning is
nigh.

Be near me, Lord Jesus, I ask thee to stay
Close by me forever, and love me, I pray;
Bless all the dear children in thy tender
care,
And fit us for heaven to live with thee
there.

shown great mercy to her, and they rejoiced with her. And on the eighth day they came to circumcise the child; and they

Go Tell It on the Mountain

Go tell it on the mountain,
Over the hills and everywhere,
Go tell it on the mountain,
That Jesus Christ is born.

When I was a seeker,
I sought both night and day,
I asked the Lord to help me,
And He showed me the Way.

He made me a watchman,
Upon a city wall,
And if I am a Christian,
I am the least of all.

Go tell it on the mountain,
Over the hills and everywhere,
Go tell it on the mountain,
That Jesus Christ is born.

Joy to the World

Joy to the world! the Lord is come;
Let earth receive her King;
Let every heart prepare Him room,
And heav'n and nature sing,
And heav'n and nature sing,
And heav'n, and heav'n and nature sing.

Joy to the earth! the Savior reigns;
Let men their songs employ;
While fields and floods,
Rocks, hills and plains,
Repeat the sounding joy,
Repeat the sounding joy,
Repeat, repeat the sounding joy.

No more let sins and sorrows grow,
Nor thorns infest the ground;
He comes to make His blessing flow
Far as the curse is found,
Far as the curse is found,
Far as, far as the curse is found.

He rules the world with truth and grace,
And makes the nations prove
The glories of His righteousness,
And wonders of His love,
And wonders of His love,
And wonders, wonders of His love.

Rise Up, Shepherd, and Follow

There's a star in the East on Christmas
   morn,
Rise up, shepherd, and follow.
It will lead to the place where the Savior's
   born,
Rise up, shepherd, and follow.

Refrain
Follow, follow,
Rise up, shepherd, and follow.
Follow the star of Bethlehem.
Rise up, shepherd, and follow.

Leave your sheep and leave your lambs.
Rise up, shepherd, and follow.
Leave your ewes and leave your rams.
Rise up, shepherd, and follow.

Refrain
Follow, follow,
Rise up, shepherd, and follow.
Follow the star of Bethlehem.
Rise up, shepherd, and follow.

If you take good heed to the angel's words.
Rise up, shepherd, and follow.
You'll forget your flocks; you'll forget your
   herds.
Rise up, shepherd, and follow.

Refrain
Follow, follow,
Rise up, shepherd, and follow.
Follow the star of Bethlehem.
Rise up, shepherd, and follow.

The First Nowell

The first Nowell the angel did say,
Was to certain poor shepherds in fields as
   they lay;
In fields where they lay keeping their
   sheep,
On a cold winter's night that was so deep.
  Nowell, Nowell, Nowell, Nowell,
  Born is the King of Israel.

For all to see there was a star
Shining in the east, beyond them far,
And to the earth it gave great light,
And so it continued both day and night.
  Nowell, Nowell, Nowell, Nowell,
  Born is the King of Israel.

And by the light of that same star
The Wise Men came from country far;
To seek for a king was their intent,
And to follow the star wherever it went.
  Nowell, Nowell, Nowell, Nowell,
  Born is the King of Israel.

Then let us all with one accord
Sing praises to our heavenly Lord
Who hath made heav'n and earth of
   naught,
And with his blood mankind hath bought.
  Nowell, Nowell, Nowell, Nowell,
  Born is the King of Israel.

It Came upon the Midnight Clear

It came upon the midnight clear,
That glorious song of old,
From angels bending near the earth,
To touch their harps of gold:
"Peace on the earth, good will to men,"
From heav'n's all gracious King.
The world in solemn stillness lay,
To hear the angels sing.

Yet with the woes of sin and strife
The world has suffered long,
Beneath the angel strain have rolled
Two thousand years of wrong;
And man, at war with man, hears not
The love song which they bring:
O hush the noise, ye men of strife,
And hear the angels sing!

All ye, beneath life's crushing load,
Whose forms are bending low,
Who toil along the climbing way
With painful steps and slow,
Look now! for glad and golden hour
Come swiftly on the wing:
O rest beside the weary road,
And hear the angels sing!

For lo! the days are hast'ning on,
By prophet bards foretold,
When with the evercircling years
Comes round the age of gold;
When peace shall over all the earth
Its ancient splendors fling,
And the whole world give back the song
Which now the angels sing.

Singing Christmas Carols

It's said that singing is "praying twice". (CCC 2652–60.) Certainly it is a beautiful way to express faith, devotion and love of God.

Singing Advent hymns and Christmas carols honors the Savior, the Infant of Bethlehem, His (and our) Blessed Mother and Saint Joseph. It's also a great way to pray together as a family.

Going carolling brings the blessings of Advent and Christmas to friends and neighbors. Singing is like a gift, a personal gift of praise and love that we give to ourselves and each other. The familiar, well-loved carols of Christmas can soften the heart and bring a smile to even the most crabby neighbor, the most atheistic friend.

A multi-family carolling party is a lot of fun. Gather in a living room with song sheets, warm drinks and cookies. You'll be surprised at the singing voices you never suspected your friends had! Once you have some practice, going out as a group tends to ease the shyness or reluctance to go door-to-door. It's easier if there is a group.

If you decide to go out carolling, carry a large cross made of two pieces of wood with a star placed in the center. Bring flashlights or lanterns to light your way and help read the song sheets. You could take donations for a charitable organization or simply sing for the love and gift of it.

"Gloria, in excelsis Deo!"

them up in their hearts, saying, "What then will this child be?" For the hand of the Lord was with him. And his father Zechariah was filled with the Holy Spirit, and

We Three Kings of Orient Are— Blessing the Home at Epiphany

The Christmas season ends with the Feast of the Epiphany. On this day, we celebrate the threefold "discovery" and manifestation of the divinity of Jesus Christ. Christ was discovered by the shepherds and the three Magi who came to worship Jesus in the manger in Bethlehem. Then He was revealed to the world during His baptism in the river Jordan by His cousin John, when the Holy Spirit in the form of a dove descended from Heaven and a voice proclaimed Him as the Son of God. Finally, He declared Himself and His ministry with His first miracle—changing water into wine during the wedding feast at Cana. Epiphany is a fitting conclusion to the most joyous season of the year. (CCC 438, 528, 535, 1668.)

In many countries Epiphany is celebrated on January 6, on whatever day of the week that falls on. In some countries it is celebrated on the first Sunday after January 1. (This is determined by the Conference of Bishops of each country.) Follow whatever suits your family schedule. Commemorate Epiphany more than once if you want, using one of our suggestions each time. You may want to hold an Epiphany party, as described later in this chapter.

There are many ways to celebrate the Feast of the Epiphany in the domestic church. The three Wise Men—which in our home are small cloth figures made of bright cloth embellished with gold braid, ribbon and shiny buttons—who have been slowly moving through the dining room toward the crèche on the living room bookcase, finally reach the manger on this night and bow before the Christ Child.

The crèche is surrounded by candles, and the tiny cloth figure of the Baby Jesus is "enthroned", with the manger draped with a scrap of purple cloth and a small crown placed on His head.

> "Behold, the Lord, the Ruler is come, the Kingdom is in His Hand, and power and dominion."

20+C+M+B+01

Then the Three Kings bless our home. Dressed as the Kings, in capes and other bright "regal" costumes with home-made crowns on our heads, we process through the house, singing "We Three Kings of Orient Are". Dad leads the way with a stick of chalk and a small bottle of holy water. At each doorway leading to the outside, we stop and he marks the lintel with:

20 + C + M + B + 01

(the numbers change each year).

He then sprinkles the doorway with holy water and says this prayer: "O Lord, grant that the names of Thy saints Caspar, Melchior and Balthazar may, through their merits and petitions, bless our home and bring physical health and spiritual protection for all who enter here. Amen."

When we have blessed our home, we begin to take down the Christmas decorations and pack them away for another year. But with the blessing of our home, we have not put away the message and promise of Christmas to be forgotten until December of next year. We have ensured that it will follow us throughout the rest of the liturgical year celebrated in our domestic church.

Another explanation for the letters C+M+B is that they represent "Christus mansionem benedicat" or "May Christ bless this house."

This is the form used in Germany, where, every year around Epiphany, children go from house to house dressed up as the Three Kings to sing and collect a special offering for children's ministries. Before they go on to the next house, they write the blessing on the door, where it remains for the remainder of the year. This explanation makes a little more sense than calling on the apocryphal names of the Wise Men.

Regardless of which explanation you choose, how you decide to observe the feast day and how elaborate you make your house-blessing ceremony, don't pass it over. It is a powerful expression and demonstration of faith to your children and the world.

Another Idea

For more information about blessing your home and holy water, look at the article about holy water on page 53.

Christmas Gifts

Ancient Romans exchanged gifts on New Year's Day. In French Canada and Scotland, this custom of giving gifts on New Year's Eve has been preserved. Depending on the wealth of the gift giver, Roman gifts varied from jewelry, pieces of gold and silver to homemade pastry, cookies and candies. Other customary gifts were gloves or the money to purchase them. This became known as "glove money". Eventually, this custom extended to metal pins (a luxury item) introduced in the sixteenth century. Eventually "pin money" came to mean the little bit of cash that women were allowed to spend as they pleased! Sweet things were given to ensure sweetness for the year to come; lamps to wish for light and warmth; and money was given to wish for increasing wealth.

The custom of giving gifts at Christmas is one of the many instances where Holy Mother Church baptized an existing custom. When the apostles brought the Gospel to Rome, the people learned of the Three Wise Men who came from the Orient to present gifts to the newborn King. As Christianity spread, the old custom changed to fit. The exchanging of presents remained (after all, who would want to give up gifts?!), but now it was done in imitation of the Three Holy Kings.

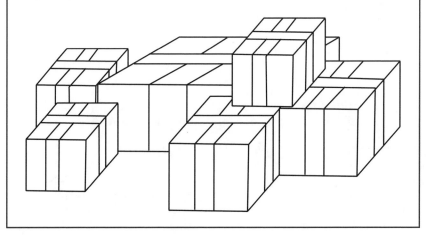

swore to our father Abraham, to grant us that we, being delivered from the hand of our enemies, might serve him without fear, in holiness and righteousness before him all

of all who hate us; to perform the mercy promised to our fathers, and to remember his holy covenant, the oath which he

Have an Epiphany Party!

If we enter into the spirit of celebrating the liturgical seasons and feasts of the Church in their proper time, then we really cannot celebrate Christmas before December 25. Advent is a season of waiting, a penitential season and should be observed with some fasting and charitable acts. The Christmas Day dinner should begin a time of feasting and celebration, not end it.

Of course, it might be difficult to convince your boss or your mother-in-law that the Christmas party should take place after Christmas rather than in the weeks before. Instead, try changing your own party-giving traditions, and hold your own traditional Christmas celebrations in the days and weeks after Christmas. A friend of mine hosts a Christmas carolling party on December 28. We bring cookies, cakes and other Christmas goodies, and she prepares hot chocolate and spiced apple juice. The children play while the adults chat, then we all gather in her living room to sing our favorite Christmas carols. It's a wonderful evening that we all look forward to.

Another opportunity for a Christmas season celebration is an Epiphany party. The main idea of any party is to get a lot of friends together to have some fun. An Epiphany party is no different. The Feast of the Epiphany and the idea of discovery or "manifestation" can provide some theme ideas for activities, food and games or crafts. A party for adults could serve filled crepes or ravioli for dinner and play charades as entertainment.

A party for families is even easier and lots of fun! Invite your friends over for the afternoon and an early potluck dinner.

Organizing a Potluck Dinner

Before you invite people, draw up a tentative menu, keeping in mind how many people are coming and what ages. Plan on at least two main course dishes to give people a choice. Then when you're inviting everyone over, suggest a specific dish to each guest. Though it may seem a bit bossy, it is actually a courtesy to your guests because it saves them the trouble

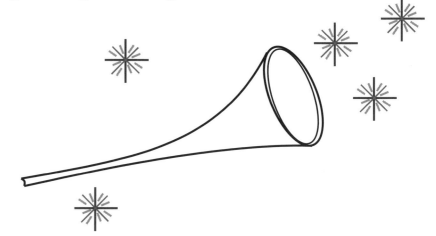

of deciding what to prepare and ensures that you have a complete meal to serve your guests.

You don't end up with three salads and no main course. As hostess, you supply paper plates, cups, napkins and disposable cutlery, and beverages.

An Epiphany Craft

As everyone gathers in the afternoon (at 2:30 P.M. or thereabouts, depending on nap times) have a big area cleared for the kids to play in. They'll mostly entertain themselves, but a few toys that encourage cooperative playing (wooden blocks, Lego, beanbags or small cars) will start the games off. This works well for the under-ten crowd. Older kids can have a play space of their own, maybe in one of the bedrooms, or some special activities set aside just for them. The simple angels or other activities from the craft section of this book would work well.

While the children play, moms can take time to chat and visit. When everyone seems to be getting a little bored (which can take quite a long time because as families and more children arrive, the playing just gets better and better), call the kids together for the main activity. Everyone gets to make a crown!

You will need:

- strips of bristol board in white, yellow and gray cut into crown shapes, one for each guest (Prepare these ahead of time.)

- small glue bottles, one for every three children

- decorations: beads, sparkles, ribbon, crayons, markers, a hole punch, macaroni and whatever else you can think of

- a stapler to close the crown around the child's head after it has been decorated and has dried

Depending on the space available and the number of children present, try to set up several stations or areas for groups of two or three children. Smaller children will need help and supervision. This is easier to manage if you've got the supplies separated a bit.

Equip each station with a glue bottle or pot and small bowls or dishes of decorations. Everyone can share and reach easily that way. The girls will dive right in, smaller children and boys may need more encouragement to spend some time decorating their crowns. But once they get the idea, they can be quite talented and creative!

As each child finishes his crown, mark it somewhere with his initials and set it aside to dry. As the children finish their crowns, let them get back to playing if they're tired of crafts. If they want to do more, give them some coloring sheets photocopied from the coloring section of this book (also available as PDF on the Domestic-Church.com web site). They can color and embellish them with glue and glitter.

Time to Eat

By this time, it's probably close to 4 or 5 o'clock. Husbands (invite them to join you after work) may be arriving, and children are starting to get hungry! Again, depending on the space available, set out the potluck dishes on a counter or table so that people can serve themselves. Moms can serve their younger

children, older ones can serve themselves. It generally works well to let the children eat first by themselves and then return to playing!

After the children have finished, the adults can sit down and eat in a somewhat quieter atmosphere.

An essential part of any party is dessert, and for an Epiphany party that means Epiphany Cake!

Epiphany Cake is any favorite cake with small treasures hidden inside. There is a more detailed explanation and some easy recipes for cake and frosting on the next page.

Heading Home

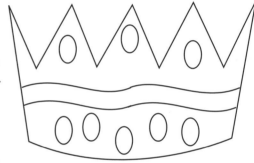

By now, it's getting close to evening and bedtimes.

Take a few minutes to staple everyone's crown closed. Wrap the crown around the child's head, centered on the forehead and just over the ears. Hold it together as you remove it from the child's head and staple it together. Put the closed crown back on the mini-King's head and watch him beam!

Time to head home. The children will be tired and happy after an afternoon of playing (well, maybe not the young teens, but then, it's not cool to admit you've had a good time, so who knows?), and the parents have had a nice chat and visit.

It's a nice idea to have pieces of chalk (the kind sold as "sidewalk chalk" is perfect), small bottles of holy water and prayer sheets to distribute to the guests as they leave so they can bless their homes. Kind of like grown-up loot bags. The children take home their crowns, of course.

Epiphany Cake

There are many traditions surrounding Epiphany. In some European countries, a very popular tradition involves hiding small items in a cake. On the night before the Feast of Epiphany, a special cake is served with three beans hidden inside, two white beans and one black one. The finders of the beans are the Kings at the Epiphany feast. Dressed in fine robes, they preside over the feast and before leaving hand out small gifts, representing gold, frankincense and myrrh.

In the royal courts of the Middle Ages, Epiphany cakes would contain a bean for the King and a pea for the Queen. Whoever found the bean and the pea would be the King and Queen of the feast.

A traditional "Christ Cake" is popular in many countries of the world. A tiny statue of Christ is baked into the cake. Whoever finds the statue is considered especially blessed throughout the coming year.

Two Epiphany Cakes

White Cake

Ingredients

2¼ cups white flour
1½ cups sugar
3 teaspoons baking powder
1 teaspoon salt
½ cup shortening
¾ cup milk
1½ teaspoons vanilla
¼ cup milk
2 eggs
dried beans, coins wrapped in foil or small figure (not plastic!)

Directions

Preheat oven to 350° F. Grease lightly and flour two 8 x 8-inch cake pans or one 9 x 13-inch pan.

Mix together the flour, sugar, baking powder and salt in a large bowl.

Drop in the shortening. Pour in the first quantity of milk and vanilla.

Mix at medium speed with an electric mixer until well blended.

Add the remainder of the milk and the eggs; beat for 2 minutes. Add beans, coins or small figure, and stir gently.

Pour into the pan or pans and bake for 25 minutes.

Cool in pan for 10 minutes, and turn out onto a cake rack, or serve from the pan.

Easy White Icing

Ingredients

¼ cup butter, melted and cooled
¼ cup cream
2 teaspoons vanilla
3 cups icing sugar, sifted to remove lumps

Directions

Combine butter, cream and vanilla in a large mixing bowl.

Slowly add sugar until the icing is thick, smooth and spreadable. Add more sugar or a few drops of cream to get the desired consistency.

Spread on cool cake.

to give light to those who sit in darkness and in the shadow of death, to guide our feet into the way of peace." And the

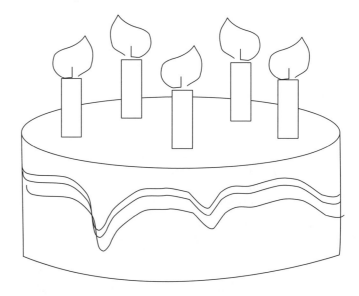

Chocolate Cake

Ingredients

½ cup unsweetened cocoa
1 cup hot strong coffee (instant coffee can be used)
½ cup shortening
1½ cups sugar
2 eggs
1 teaspoon vanilla
1½ cups white flour
¾ teaspoon salt
¼ teaspoon baking powder
1 teaspoon baking soda
dried beans, coins wrapped in foil or small figure (not plastic!)

Directions

Preheat oven to 350° F. Grease lightly and flour two 8-inch round cake pans.

Combine the cocoa and hot coffee in a small bowl or cup; mix well and set aside.

Put the shortening, sugar, eggs and vanilla in a large mixing bowl and beat until they are light and fluffy.

Stir or sift together the flour, salt, baking powder and baking soda.

Add a third of the dry ingredients to the shortening and egg mixture; blend in.

Add half the cocoa mixture to the batter. Mix in.

Repeat with dry ingredients, then remaining cocoa mixture, ending with dry ingredients, blending well after each addition so that the batter is smooth and evenly chocolate colored.

Add beans, coins or small figure, and stir gently.

Pour into prepared cake pans and bake for 25 minutes until a toothpick inserted in the center comes out clean, with a few fudgy bits sticking to it.

Allow to cool in the pans for 5 minutes and turn out onto racks to cool completely.

Easy Chocolate Icing

Ingredients

6 ounces semisweet chocolate (either squares or chips)
½ cup sour cream
⅛ teaspoon salt

Directions

Melt the chocolate over simmering water or in a microwave oven.

Add the sour cream and salt and stir until thoroughly blended.

Spread on cool cake while icing is still warm.

there, the time came for her to be delivered. And she gave birth to her first-born son and wrapped him in swaddling cloths, and laid him in a manger, because there was no place

Hidden Life—Forcing Bulbs

In the depths of winter, spring seems a very long time away. In the long darkness of the first Advent, between the Fall of Man and the Birth of Christ, the coming of the promised Messiah seemed at times as if it would never happen. The three days between the Crucifixion and the Resurrection must have seemed long and empty to Christ's faithful followers, even if they did remember His promises, though the Gospels indicate that they did not.

A dark and dreary winter day is a good time to teach the family about the return of spring and hope. We can also use the "hiding" (planting) of bulbs to illustrate vividly both the hidden years of Christ's life in Nazareth and the hidden lost hopes of the buried Christ. What a miracle when He rose from the dead!

If you follow a few simple principles, forcing bulbs is a very easy procedure. Most bulbs need a period of dormancy and cold to prepare a good root and to trigger development of the flower head. It is possible to buy bulbs that have been cold treated, or you can plant them in earth and cold treat them yourself.

"Forcing"—coaxing, actually—is the term used to describe the process to get bulbs to bloom out of season. Among the most commonly forced and easiest bulb flowers are amaryllis, paperwhite narcissus, muscari and hyacinths. Spring-flowering bulbs usually require a rooting period of about twelve to fifteen weeks (three to four months) at temperatures between 41 and 48° F in order to produce a good root system, which is essential if they are to be "forced" into flower.

Potting Bulbs for Cooling/Rooting

Use clean pots with drainage holes (the depth will depend on the bulbs being grown). Allow for two inches of soil below the bulb and select a pot large enough to allow the top of the bulb to be even with the rim when placed on the soil. Plain potting soil is fine. You can add some bone meal or special fertilizer formulated for bulbs, just a pinch per bulb, to the soil mixture.

Place two inches of soil in the pot, then place (don't push) bulbs into position. Add enough soil to fill the pot, firming the soil gently around the bulbs, being careful not to bruise them. Water well in order to settle the soil around the bulbs. Bulbs can be planted very close together, even touching, and they make the best show in crowded arrangements.

Storing the Planted Bulbs

Remember, if the bulbs were outside planted in the ground, they would be protected from freezing by the soil. So, in the house, they need to be stored in a cool but not cold place. After potting your bulbs, store them in a cool place, such as an old (functioning) refrigerator, a root cellar or cool basement, or in the garage if outdoor temperatures stay below 45° F but above freezing. Vegetable or crisper drawers can be used, but don't store bulbs in the same drawer with ripening fruit or vegetables. They give off ethylene gas, which can harm the bulbs. Besides, the bulbs can take up an incredible amount of space in your already crowded refrigerator. To keep the bulbs dark, place the pots in paper grocery sacks and staple the tops shut. Since some bulbs are poisonous, this storage method will also help keep young children away from the bulbs.

Different types of bulbs require differing periods of time to root well. For this reason it doesn't work well to combine different types of bulbs in the same pot. Label each paper bag with the name of the variety, planting date, and the date you intend to bring it out of storage for forcing.

Bringing Them to Flower

Bulbs will flower some three to four weeks after they have been brought into warmer temperatures. Thus, from time of planting to flowering, allow a period of fifteen weeks, comprised of twelve weeks for rooting, then three weeks in warmer temperatures to flower. It is easier to hold bulbs back than to speed them up, so when you know the date you want them to be in flower, calculate accordingly the best planting time. (For Easter season flowers, for example, plant bulbs in early to mid-January—just at the end of Epiphany, in fact.)

Forcing Blooms

Now that the cooling stage is finished, the "forcing" begins. The forcing begins at the stage when you remove the bulbs from the root-growing cool environment into warmth and light, triggering the growth of leaves and flowers. Sunshine and temperature are the most important factors in promoting successful flowering. Most bulbs will require about three or four weeks from the time they are removed from cold storage before they bloom. So remove the pots from the cool place on the Fourth Sunday of Lent.

First put the pots in a place indoors with indirect sunlight and temperatures about 60° F for a week or two. When the shoots are four to six inches tall, move the pots to a bright, sunny window to stimulate blooming. A temperature of about 68° F and direct sunlight will produce the best results. When the buds take on color, return the plants to indirect sunlight to make the blossoms last. Keep the soil moist at all times.

Easy Paper-White Narcissus

Paper-whites (*narcissus tazetta*) are among the most popular forcing flowers that don't require the twelve-week rooting period. Paper-whites are most often (and most easily) potted in shallow containers of gravel. Place bulbs on a layer of gravel and carefully fill in enough gravel to hold bulbs but not cover them. A crowded grouping will be the most attractive.

It is best to cool containers, at temperatures between 45 and 50° F, preferably in an area with low light or complete darkness. The refrigerator is good for this too. Keep containers cooled for about three weeks or until roots are well formed (this can be seen easily when bulbs are set in gravel). Then move into a sunny spot for forcing.

The Easiest Bulbs for Forcing

1. Paper-white narcissus; popular bulb; grows in soil or gravel.
2. Amaryllis; popular Christmas plant (plant bulb in early November, no cooling necessary).
3. Large-flowering crocus; requires twelve- to fourteen-week rooting period; bulbs can be potted in gravel and water for different effect.
4. Hyacinth; fragrant springtime favorite; requires about twelve weeks for rooting; can be forced in special "hyacinth" vases using only water.
5. Colchicum; excellent for forcing, can even grow on a windowsill without soil or water; begins blooming in about two weeks.
6. Muscari; requires sixteen-week rooting time; pot plenty, they're small.
7. Iris; *iris reticulata*, especially, are easy to force, but need careful attention to drainage; require about fifteen weeks for rooting; don't hold iris bulbs too long before potting; tall-stemmed iris are less suited to forcing.
8. Daffodils require very bright light, such as that found in a greenhouse, to flower well. Too little sun results in leggy growth and no blossoms. Only the miniature varieties (hybrid) of daffodils are recommended for home forcing. Daffodils usually require a twelve- to fourteen-week rooting period. Once removed from the rooting area, daffodils must be placed in a location that receives lots of sun, such as an enclosed porch, a sunroom or under a skylight.

With this planting and then waiting, bringing into the light and finally the miraculous flowering, a message will be brought to life for the whole family. Even in the darkest times, with the least sign of life and hope, God's Love is there waiting for us to find it and bring it into the open.

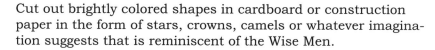

Celebrating Epiphany with Spiritual Gifts

Coming as it does at the first of the New Year, Epiphany is an opportunity to recognize what the coming of the Messiah means for the world. The gift of our Savior brings new hope to us all. He is the fulfillment of prophecy, the gift of our loving Father, the bringer of unlimited graces for those who believe and trust in Him.

We receive these gifts from the Holy Spirit and the Christ Child throughout the year. (CCC 694–701.) Why not include a celebration of these gifts in our celebration of Epiphany?

This simple tradition brings the spiritual gifts of the Christ Child to life for the family and helps the little ones learn how closely our spiritual life touches our material lives.

Cut out brightly colored shapes in cardboard or construction paper in the form of stars, crowns, camels or whatever imagination suggests that is reminiscent of the Wise Men.

On each piece write a word or phrase. These could be single-word virtues, such as:

faith, hope, charity, fortitude, patience.

Phrases could suggest a quality of soul, such as:

a spirit of cheerfulness, simplicity of faith, open-heartedness, or childlike faith.

Put all the pieces into a basket or jar and mix them up well. At evening prayers, after the family has said a short prayer asking the Holy Spirit to guide their choice, let every family member pick out a card. He should not look while choosing; the choice should be "random". What each person gets will be a surprise and a delight!

Throughout the remainder of the year, the recipients should remember and exercise their particular gifts in the work of daily living. Perhaps the cards could stay at the family altar, or be stuck under the casing of a doorway or window, or decorate the mirror of each person's bedroom. It should be placed where it can be seen and noticed each day.

Saints of the Season

lying in a manger. And when they saw it they made known the saying which had been told them concerning this child; and all who heard it wondered at what the shepherds

Celebrating Saint Nicholas Day

Special patron of children
Feast day: December 6

"You better watch out, you better not cry. You better not pout, I'm telling you why, Santa Claus is coming to town." The whole notion of Santa Claus bringing presents and excitement and socially sanctioned greed is the main distraction for families trying to celebrate the miracle of the Incarnation. Why not solve the problem by figuratively sealing off your chimney, uninviting Santa, as it were? Extend an invitation to Saint Nicholas in his stead.

The feast day of Saint Nicholas is nearly three weeks before Christmas, neatly separating the solemnity of Christmas from the gifts and toys bonanza atmosphere of Santa Claus. (An added benefit is that Saint Nicholas has never heard of the Ninja Turtles, Pokémon or anything else that is advertised on TV!)

A saint in Heaven, a good bishop who lived long ago and is now praying for us, makes more sense to children anyway than some strange story about a fat gentleman who comes down chimneys even when there is not a chimney on the house. You never have to grow out of believing in Saint Nicholas either. (See CCC 956–57, 2030, 2683–84.)

Invite Saint Nicholas into Your Home

So it is Saint Nicholas who visits our home and leaves gifts in our stockings. On the evenings of December 3, 4 and 5 during our evening prayers, we say prayers to Saint Nicholas, thanking him for his continued guidance and intercession. We hang our stockings as part of the evening prayer ritual on December 5. Since we do not have a fireplace, we hang our stockings on the breakfast table chairs.

On that evening, we also set the table for breakfast. We use a red tablecloth, bring out the best silver and plates and decorate the table with candles and anything else that strikes our imagination—candles, small statues, a scattering of

oranges and chocolate money, pine boughs. It is always beautiful. Then I bake a coffee cake, cut grapefruit and get the juice and coffeepot ready for a very early morning feast!

(When our children were younger, they would hang their stockings just before going to bed. Otherwise, the suspense would be too much.)

Gifts from Saint Nicholas

In the middle of the night, a mysterious someone fills everyone's stockings. "Stocking gifts" are never large or expensive. Rarely does any one item cost more than $10. They don't need to. This is the celebration of a feast day, not an occasion to get "stuff". And they are not competing for attention with the Christmas gift from Grandma.

Typically, stockings in our house contain a book, a tangerine, some chocolate money, a new pen or penknife, a small toy or new CD. A nice piece of handmade jewelry from a craft fair, a new tool from the hardware store, or a package of special teas are other possibilities. After a few years of direct hints, Mom even gets some real surprises in her stocking.

The children adapted very quickly and easily to the new, smaller stockings when we began our tradition of celebrating Saint Nicholas Day, probably because, though the presents were small, the children received presents three weeks before their school friends did.

A Wonderful Family Tradition

The morning of December 6 always starts very early, usually around 5 o'clock, when an avalanche of excited children lands on our bed. (They sleep a little later now that they are blasé

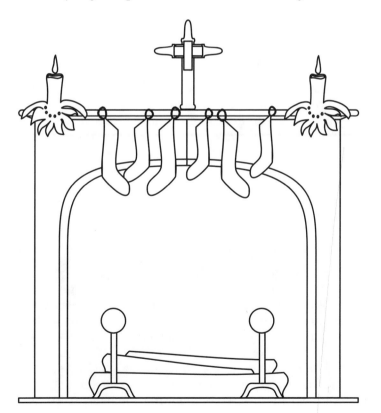

teens. But not much!) There is plenty of time to eat and talk before school and work starts. (If need be, I drive them to school that day.) We have a feast for breakfast and empty our stockings as we eat.

In the early morning of December 6, as the dawn slowly stains the sky pink and lights the snow, it is really pleasant to relax and enjoy the children's chatter without worrying about cooking a turkey and getting to Mass on time or wondering whether stocking gifts are distracting them from the Nativity. In the evening, we thank Saint Nicholas for his gifts and ask him to continue to pray for us in the coming year.

Peter and I have heard few regrets from the children about the passing of Santa Claus. We have none. Taking Santa Claus out of Christmas, and taking the silly red elf suit off Saint Nicholas, has been the best thing we could have done to reclaim the Nativity, to teach our children about giving and receiving, and actually to enjoy Christmas.

Who Is Saint Nicholas?

The character of Santa Claus is copied from the life of a real person, a saint named Nicholas. The name "Saint Nicholas" even sounds like "San-ta Claus", especially in the Dutch language. The Dutch celebration of "Sinter Klaus" was brought to North America with the Dutch settlers and eventually became the legend of Santa Claus, complete with reindeer, elves and bottomless gift bags. The real story of the saint is much more inspiring.

The Real Story of Saint Nicholas

Saint Nicholas is the patron of seafarers, scholars, bankers, pawnbrokers, jurists, brewers, coopers, travelers, perfumers, unmarried girls, brides, schoolboys and—robbers. But he is most famous as the special patron of children.

Saint Nicholas was probably a native of Patara, in Lycia, Asia Minor. There are far more legends about his miraculous good deeds than there are clear details about his life. The good Nicholas has been widely honored as a saint since the sixth century. No fewer than twenty-one miracles are attributed to him. He became known for his holiness, zeal and astonishing miracles. Besides that, this is known for sure: Nicholas was first a monk in the monastery of Holy Zion near Myra. Eventually he was made Abbot by the archbishop who was its founder.

Nicholas also apparently studied at Alexandria, Egypt. At the time, it was an important center of learning. On one of his voyages there he is said to have saved the life of a sailor who fell from the ship's rigging in a storm. Remembrance of this act caused him to became the patron saint of sailors. Later, he miraculously rescued some young boys from a vat of brine. (One wonders what the boys were doing in the brine. One version of the legend says that they were murdered and their bodies hidden there. No matter; the act caused him to be named patron saint of schoolboys.)

While visiting the Turkish town of Myra, Nicholas entered the local church to give thanks for a safe voyage. He did not know that the elders of the See of Myra, capital of Lycia, could not agree on a successor to their recently deceased archbishop. According to the legend they had been counseled in a dream to choose the next person named Nicholas (which means "victory" in Greek) who visited the church. So it was that Nicholas became known as Bishop of Myra, worker of miracles and benefactor of the poor. Legends also state that he was present at the Council of Nicaea as an opponent of Arianism. Nicholas suffered for the faith under the emperor Diocletian. His death occurred at Myra, in the year 342.

Saint Nicholas' best-known virtue was his love and charity for the poor. Because of this and of the many legends of his works, Saint Nicholas is the special patron of children. He is among the most popular saints of the Church. More than twelve hundred churches are named in his honor (nearly four hundred churches in England); and he is said to have been represented by Christian artists more frequently than any saint except Our Lady. He has always been honored with great veneration in the Latin and Greek Churches. The Russian Church seems to honor him more than any other saint after the apostles.

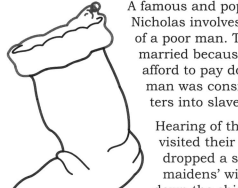

A famous and popular legend about Saint Nicholas involves three unwed daughters of a poor man. The maidens could not get married because their father could not afford to pay dowries. In despair, the man was considering selling his daughters into slavery or prostitution.

Hearing of their plight, Saint Nicholas visited their house late one night and dropped a small bag of gold in the maidens' window (some versions say down the chimney). The eldest daughter married. In the ensuing months, he dropped in a second bag of gold, then a third. On one of the nights, the gold landed in a stocking hung up to dry. From this detail, the tradition of leaving gifts in stockings was born.

After two of his daughters had been able to marry because of the money mysteriously appearing in their stockings, their father was determined to find out who was helping them, so he hid behind the chimney the next night. Along came Bishop Nicholas with another bag of money. When Nicholas was discovered, he asked the father not to tell anyone else, but the father wanted everyone to know what a good and generous man the Bishop Nicholas was, so he told everyone he knew. The story persisted and Nicholas was thereafter honored as patron saint of unwed maidens. This story was told for so many generations that the theme of the three bags of gold, or gold balls, was adopted as a symbol by bankers and moneylenders.

In honor of the saint, children have traditionally received a visit from their patron on his feast day. He brings them gifts of candies, cookies, apples or nuts. In some places, the children put their shoes on the windowsill on the eve of Saint Nicholas' Day and find them filled with candies, cookies, oranges and dried fruit the next morning. In Holland, gifts were left in the children's wooden shoes. In convent boarding schools, the young women students would leave their stockings at the door of their abbess' room, with notes recommending themselves to the generosity of Saint Nicholas—the forerunner of letters to Santa Claus. The next morning the abbess would summon her charges and show them their stockings filled—supposedly by Saint Nicholas—with sweetmeats.

In some European countries, gifts are exchanged on Saint Nicholas Day rather than on Christmas. A charming story from Russia explains that the Infant Jesus, being far too young to travel around the world in one night, asks Saint Nicholas to bring gifts to good children on His behalf in celebration of His birth. Saint Nicholas, of course, is happy to obey.

Prayer

We call upon your mercy, O Lord. Through the intercession of Saint Nicholas, keep us safe amid all dangers so that we may go forward without hindrance on the road of salvation. Amen.

D'ou viens-tu, Bergère?

(A seventeenth-century Christmas carol from Quebec)

D'ou viens tu, bergère,
D'ou viens tu?
Je viens de l'étable,
De m'y promener;
J'ai vu un miracle,
Ce soir arrivé.

Qu'as tu vu, bergère,
Qu'as tu vu?
J'ai vu dans la crèche,
Un petit Enfant,
Sur la paille fraîche,
Mis bien tendrement.

Rien de plus, bergère,
Rien de plus?
Saint' Marie, sa mère,
Lui fait boir' du lait,
Saint Joseph, son père,
Qui tremble de froid.

Rien de plus, bergère,
Rien de plus?
Ya le boeuf et l'ane,
Qui sont par devant;
Avec leur haleine,
Réchauffent l'Enfant.

Rien de plus, bergère,
Rien de plus?
Ya trois petits ange,
Descendus du ciel,
Chantant les louanges,
Du Père Eternel.

"I Am the Immaculate Conception"

Honoring Mary, the Mother of Jesus
Solemnity: December 8

The Feast of the Immaculate Conception honors the miraculous beginnings of Mary's life. She was chosen to be the Mother of God at the moment of her conception. (CCC 490–94, 503.) What an amazing thought!

This feast is a perfect opportunity to review (or reveal) the wonders of conception and pregnancy with our children. We can instill a real sense of reverence for life and its beginnings in our children and our families through observance of this feast. We can also reinforce respect for our bodies, made by God for great and holy things. (This message, of course, is in direct contradiction to the "I have the right to decide what happens to *my* body" notion, so popular and damaging. It isn't necessary to refer to or attack the popular pro-choice position; your teaching, and living, of truth will reveal its errors quite effectively.) (CCC 2319.)

Read the Gospel of the Annunciation out loud at some point during the day, maybe at mid-afternoon quiet time or during dinner. Read a story of Mary's life or the following story about the apparition at Lourdes too. (There are many beautiful children's books about Mary available.) Use the ideas introduced in these stories to discuss God's miraculous plans for Mary and for us.

Make this "Treat a Pregnant Lady" day. There are so many small things we can do to make life a little easier for a pregnant mom, from taking the toddlers for the day to providing a few frozen casseroles. Use your imagination, and enlist your children's help in creating a surprise. (CCC 1822.)

If you don't know a pregnant lady, how about putting together some gift packages of maternity or baby clothes, nice toiletries or baby necessities and delivering them to the local home for unwed mothers or a pregnancy crisis center? The packages don't need to be elaborate or expensive; homemade stuffed toys or simple basic toiletries are needed and appreciated by these organizations. Again, enlist the children's ideas and

help to put the packages together. Wrap them up nicely with attractive paper and a bow. A young woman feeling very scared and alone in the world will gain immeasurable good by the message that someone out there honors her for carrying new life to term. The Feast of the Immaculate Conception provides a great opportunity to transform faith and teaching into good works.

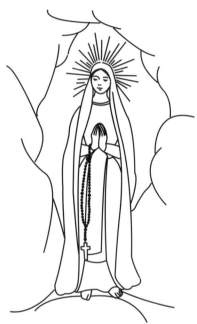

White Food for the Feast

At a feast observing the spotless nature of Mary's soul, a meal of all white food seems appropriate (and really simple!). Serve rice or mashed potatoes, plain broiled chicken or fish, coleslaw made with white winter cabbage and vinaigrette, glasses of milk and water for the adults to drink. A white cake or an angel food cake with White Mountain frosting for dessert completes the All-White Feast.

The Apparition at Lourdes

On February 11, 1858, one of the most famous of all Mary's apparitions began. Our Lady appeared to a fourteen-year-old peasant girl named Bernadette Soubirous.

She was the oldest daughter of one of the poorest families in the town. Bernadette was sickly and had to be kept from the cold and from working too hard. Despite this, she was allowed one day to go collecting firewood with two friends. She and her friends passed by the rock of Massabielle (big rock, in the local dialect), a craggy outcropping in a wild and deserted part of the countryside.

After a little while, Bernadette's friends decided to cross the river that ran near the rock. The water was cold, and Bernadette didn't want to get her feet wet. She stayed on the other side for a while and then sat down to take off her shoes, because she didn't want to be left behind. Suddenly, she heard a loud noise, "like wind". Turning, she saw "a beautiful Lady" dressed in white with a rosary hanging from her arm, standing in a small cleft or grotto in the rock. The Lady smiled at her and beckoned her to approach, and they prayed the rosary together. Bernadette prayed and the Lady joined in for the Glory Be.

At first, no one believed what she had seen, and her mother said she couldn't visit the site again. Bernadette obeyed her mother. A few days later, some friends who had heard Bernadette's story asked Madame Soubirous if Bernadette could go back to the grotto. Then her mother gave permission.

On February 18, the Lady asked Bernadette to come for fifteen days. Day after day, Bernadette went to the rock and the Lady appeared. Each time, she told Bernadette a little more about who she was. More and more people went with Bernadette. They did not see the Lady, but they could tell that Bernadette was seeing something very special and beautiful, because Bernadette looked so happy and beautiful herself when the Lady was there.

The Lady told her that we all must "pray for the conversion of sinners" and do "penance, penance, penance!" She told Bernadette, "Tell the priests to have people come here in a procession and to have a chapel built here."

On February 25, two weeks after the beginning of her appearances, the Lady of the grotto made a new spring of water well up near Bernadette. The Lady told her to drink from it and wash herself in it. That spring is still there today. Many people go to visit the shrine of Our Lady of Lourdes and take away Lourdes water. Many people have been healed of all kinds of illnesses when they visited the shrine at Lourdes and either drank the water or bathed in it.

Our Lady appeared to Bernadette eighteen times. Finally, on March 25, the Lady told Bernadette, "I am the Immaculate Conception." Bernadette didn't know what these words meant, but she carefully repeated them to herself to remember them correctly. Bernadette went straight to the priest's house and said the words to the village priest. He was very surprised.

The Immaculate Conception means that Mary was created in her mother's womb and born without sin. Of course, the one who was going to be the Mother of God and carry Jesus in her womb would have to be without sin herself. Mary is the only person in the whole world, besides Jesus, who was born without Original Sin. The declaration to the Church and the world that Mary was the Immaculate Conception had been made only four years before Bernadette heard it from the Lady herself.

Since Bernadette could not have made up words that she didn't understand, it became obvious that the Lady in the grotto was the Virgin Mary herself and that the little village of Lourdes had been greatly honored by her appearances there. Many millions of people have been to Lourdes in the years since the apparition of Our Lady of Lourdes.

Prayer

Merciful God, come to the aid of our frailty. May we who keep the memory of the Immaculate Mother of God rise from our iniquities with the help of her intercession. Amen.

Our Lady of Guadalupe

Our Lady of Mexico; Patroness of the Americas
Protectress of the unborn
Feast day: December 12

In the dead of winter, we celebrate an amazing miracle when roses bloomed in December and faith sprang up like spring corn in Mexico! In Mexico on this feast day, large processions enter the beautiful basilica of Our Lady of Guadalupe near Mexico City with flowers, banners and singing meant to symbolize the singing of birds heard by Juan Diego at the first apparition of Mary. It is a special feast day for families too.

What better time to break the solemnity of Advent just a little and celebrate one of the miracles of our faith? Have everyone over for an Our Lady of Guadalupe party and share the joy of the feast day.

What's an Our Lady of Guadalupe Party?

At an Our Lady of Guadalupe party, the decorations, costumes and, of course, food all have a Mexican theme. Some people hold their parties at the parish hall for all the children of the parish. Everyone is invited to come in "Mexican" costume, and the costumes are judged for authenticity or originality. Many small Juan Diegos and Marys turn out at these parties.

If this seems too big a challenge, an Our Lady of Guadalupe party can be hosted in your home. Invite everyone from the mother's prayer group or playgroup.

Provide lots of corn chips, salsa, grated cheese, refried beans and rice, tacos, fruit juice and fresh fruit as snacks or for a buffet dinner when the games are finished. (Finger food is probably better than fork and knife food like burritos at this kind of gathering.)

This party could be a pot-luck dinner as described in Family Activities: Epiphany party on page 30. With a pot-luck dinner, you're sure to serve food that everyone—even picky children—will be happy eating.

Red, green and white streamers, brightly colored tablecloths, "God's eye" decorations and, of course, piñatas are perfect for decorations.

Games

What kind of games? In keeping with the idea of Juan Diego carrying his tilma full of roses to the bishop's house, games that involve carrying would be appropriate, for example, "Egg on a Spoon" races. Simple games for children, such as "Pin the Tail on Juan's Donkey" (this is a bit of poetic licence, as Juan probably couldn't afford a donkey) or a "Treasure Hunt for Mary's Roses", would also be lots of fun. But you must have a piñata!

Making a Piñata

Children love piñatas for several reasons.

- First, they are bright and colorful.
- Second, they are full of candy and small prizes.
- Third, normal rules of behavior encouraging sharing and gentleness are suspended, and the children are allowed to scramble for as much candy as they can reach.
- Fourth, it's something that they are allowed to break! They can hit it as hard as they want!

Piñatas are easy to make, though they require a few days and some planning ahead. This is always difficult, especially at this busy time of year, but the results are worth it! To make a good-sized piñata, you will need:

- a *large* round balloon or beach ball
- a good pile of old newspapers
- white glue or flour and water to make a paste
- scissors and a craft knife
- tape (regular or masking)
- thin cardboard
- crayons, markers, poster paint
- tissue paper or construction paper
- string or yarn
- goodies to fill the piñata—candy, of course, but also include holy cards, medals and other items

Step One

Spread newspapers or plastic sheeting over your work surface. Blow up the balloon or beach ball and tie a knot at the end. Tear newspapers into strips about 1 inch wide and about 6 inches long. Tearing rather than cutting is important; it helps the strips lie flat on top of each other. Pour some of the glue into a disposable bowl or a bowl you don't mind soaking in water for a long while, or mix flour and cold water to make a paste the consistency of thick glue. Dip the newspaper strips into the glue and spread them onto the balloon. Thoroughly cover the balloon, leaving a small hole at the top to remove the balloon and to fill the piñata. Let the first layer dry.

Step Two

Repeat step one twice more, until the papier-mâché is built up to a good thickness. Next day, if the paper feels dry when you touch it, wrap the balloon with the yarn to give it strength to hold when swinging it. Add another two layers of glue and newspapers. Let it dry for another day. Puncture and remove the balloon.

Decorating the Piñata

Traditional shapes for the piñata include donkeys (for the donkey that carried Mary), fish (symbolizing Christ) and birds (for the birds that sang when Mary appeared to Juan Diego). Roll the cardboard to make legs and a head for the donkey, then build up the shape with more papier-mâché. Shape a cone for the head and tail of a fish, then add fins and eyes. Use additional layers of papier-mâché to make it look fishlike. A similar technique will create a bird body, onto which can then be added wings, legs and a tail. A simpler piñata can be made as a ball with decorated papier-mâché cones sticking out all over it. Paper streamers hang from the cones.

When the shape is finished and dry, fill the piñata with candy and goodies, and cover the hole with a few layers of paper. Then paint the piñata. Piñatas should be bright and colorful. Crepe paper streamers cut up with a fringe can be

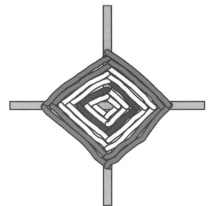

curled up with the help of a pencil and glued onto the piñata. Start from the bottom and layer them overlapping. Decorate the cones with the crepe paper, adding strings to the tips.

Playing the Piñata Game

Hang the piñata up from the ceiling. Each child gets a turn trying to break the piñata. Blindfold the child and give him or her a stick (a broom handle works well). Turn the child around in a circle two or three times and point him in the direction of the piñata. The child gets to swing the stick a prearranged number of times. Make sure everyone else stands clear of the swinging stick, including the grown-ups!

Then another child gets a turn. When someone breaks the piñata, all the children get to gather the goodies. You might want to have little paper bags, each with a child's name on it, so the children have a place to store their goodies for the remainder of the party and a way to carry everything home.

Making "God's Eye" Decorations

These simple decorations are often made at summer camps because they are bright, colorful, very easy and adaptable to all situations, supplies and skill levels. You will need:

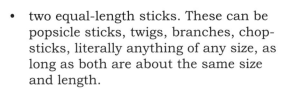

- two equal-length sticks. These can be popsicle sticks, twigs, branches, chop-sticks, literally anything of any size, as long as both are about the same size and length.

- string, yarn, strips of cloth, marking tape. Brightly colored is best, especially if you can find several different contrasting shades.

  Tie a piece of yarn in the middle of one of the sticks. Hold the other stick across the first and wrap the yarn around it, to lash the two together.

Every time the yarn crosses a stick wrap it completely around the stick before proceeding to the next stick. Go around and around the crossed sticks, gradually the yarn will fill up the space.

Change colors every once in a while to make a pattern. When you can't (or don't want to) wrap any more yarn, tie it tightly to one of the sticks. You're done.

Juan Diego and the Beautiful Lady

When we learn about the Feast of Our Lady of Guadalupe we learn about faith and we learn about understanding other people.

After Christopher Columbus discovered America, Spanish soldiers called *conquistadors* came to Mexico to conquer the country and make it part of the Spanish Empire. Missionaries came to Mexico with the *conquistadors*. The missionaries wanted to share the Word of God with the newly discovered people, to "spread the Word through all the nations" as Christ instructed. They weren't very successful at first.

After the missionaries had been in Mexico for thirty years, only a few hundred native Indios had converted to the Christian faith. No one was sure whether the natives didn't understand the new faith because it was so different from their old beliefs, or whether the Indios didn't like the *conquistadors* and so they disliked the missionaries who came with them.

Then in 1531, miracles began to happen. Jesus' own Mother appeared to humble Juan Diego, one of the few Christian converts! There were miraculous signs—roses growing on a frozen hillside, Juan's uncle miraculously cured and especially the Lady's beautiful image on Juan's mantle—teaching the people more about the truth and beauty of Christ's teaching than the missionaries had in years.

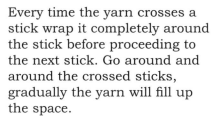

Within a short time, six million native Indios were baptized as Christians.

From this wonderful story, and the continuation of the devotion to Our Lady of Guadalupe to this day, we learn about our faith. It is clear that God has chosen Mary, the Blessed Virgin, to lead us to Jesus, her Son. The devotion and the passing on of faith that have come from the apparition to Juan Diego show this.

We also learn something from the apparition itself. Mary appeared to Blessed Juan Diego not as a European Madonna but as a beautiful Aztec princess speaking to him in his own Aztec language. Christ and Christianity are for all peoples in all ages. Even if the language is different, or the music and costumes are different, if we need to use different words and ways to teach Christ's message, the message is always the same, and always true for everyone.

Novena in Honor of Our Lady of Guadalupe

First Day   Dearest Lady of Guadalupe, fruitful Mother of holiness, teach me your ways of gentleness and strength. Hear my humble prayer offered with heartfelt confidence to beg this favor. Our Father. Hail Mary. Glory Be.

Second Day   O Mary, conceived without sin, I come to your throne of grace to share the fervent devotion of your faithful Mexican children who call to you under the glorious title of Our Lady of Guadalupe. Obtain for me a lively faith to do your Son's holy will always: May His will be done on earth as it is in Heaven. Our Father. Hail Mary. Glory Be.

Third Day   O Mary, whose Immaculate Heart was pierced by seven swords of grief, help me to walk valiantly amid the sharp thorns strewn across my pathway. Obtain for me the strength to be a true imitator of you. This I ask you, my dear Mother. Our Father. Hail Mary. Glory Be.

Fourth Day   Dearest Mother of Guadalupe, I beg you for a fortified will to imitate your divine Son's charity, to seek always the good of others in need. Grant me this, I humbly ask of you. Our Father. Hail Mary. Glory Be.

Fifth Day   O most holy Mother, I beg you to obtain for me pardon of all my sins, abundant graces to serve your Son more faithfully from now on, and lastly, the grace to praise Him with you for ever in Heaven. Our Father. Hail Mary. Glory Be.

Sixth Day   Mary, Mother of vocations, multiply priestly vocations and fill the earth with religious houses that will be light and warmth for the world, safety in stormy nights. Beg your Son to send us many priests and religious. This we ask of you, O Mother. Our Father. Hail Mary. Glory Be.

Seventh Day   O Lady of Guadalupe, we beg you that parents live a holy life and educate their children in a Christian manner; that children obey and follow the directions of their parents; that all members of the family pray and worship together. This we ask of you, O Mother. Our Father. Hail Mary. Glory Be.

Eighth Day   With my heart full of the most sincere veneration, I prostrate myself before you, O Mother, to ask you to obtain for me the grace to fulfill the duties of my state in life with faithfulness and constancy. Our Father. Hail Mary. Glory Be.

Ninth Day   O God, You have been pleased to bestow upon us unceasing favors by having placed us under the special protection of the Most Blessed Virgin Mary. Grant us, Your humble servants, who rejoice in honoring her today upon earth, the happiness of seeing her face to face in Heaven. Our Father. Hail Mary. Glory Be.

no crib for a bed, The little Lord Jesus laid down his sweet head; The stars in the sky looked down where he lay, The little

Lord Jesus, asleep on the hay. (Verse 2) The cattle are lowing, the Baby awakes, But little Lord Jesus, no crying he

The Light of Saint Lucy

Patroness of the blind
Patroness of Sicily
Feast day: December 13

Like the Feast of Saint Nicholas a week earlier, family or house-hold celebrations of Saint Lucy (or Lucia) are morning occasions. On December 13 in the dark of Swedish winter where these customs originated, a bright and shining joyous tradition like the celebration of Saint Lucy's Day makes a welcome change.

The oldest girl in the house portrays Saint Lucy, a maiden martyr. She wakes the rest of the family. (Traditionally, she's supposed to sing hymns praising Saint Lucy and Advent hymns, but in our tone-deaf household we beg people not to sing, especially early in the morning!) Dressed in a white robe, with a red sash and wearing a wire-and-greenery crown holding nine candles on her head, "Lucy" greets the sleepers with a tray of hot drinks and warm spicy buns. Called "Lucy Cats", or Lusse-katter, the buns are flavored with saffron or cardamon, though hot cross buns would be a good substitute.

Everyone has a warm bun and a hot drink and then gets up. In Sweden the rest of the day is filled with more "Lucia processions".

The basis for this tradition lies in the story of Saint Lucy. She lived in Sicily (where she is still a popular saint today) in the third century. At the time, Christians were severely persecuted by the Roman emperor Diocletian. She is said to have helped hide fellow Christians in the catacombs and underground caves. Every night, Saint Lucy would climb down into the caves to bring food to the concealed faithful. To free her hands to carry the food, she placed her oil lamp on her head. To the waiting Christians, she appeared every night out of the darkness with her head wreathed in light.

It's a beautiful image, echoed and remembered in the Swedish tradition of the "family Lucy" and Lucy Cats.

In Sicily, the little virgin martyr is honored as the patroness of the blind, because legend holds that she was blinded by her torturers. She is also celebrated as the savior of Syracuse, Sicily. According to a legend, during a great famine the Syracusans were praying for Saint Lucy's help when a ship carrying grain entered the harbor and saved the city. They eat savory or main dishes made of wheat and chickpeas (symbolizing eyeballs!) on the saint's feast day. Lucy Cats sound better, especially first thing in the morning.

Lussekatter Buns

Makes about 2 dozen buns, depending on size.

Ingredients

- saffron threads, one tube, approximately 0.5 grams
- ½ cup sugar
- 1¼ cups milk
- ½ cup butter, melted
- 1 tablespoon or small package dried yeast
- ⅛ teaspoon salt
- 1 egg, beaten
- 3¼ cups unbleached, all-purpose flour
- plus additional flour for kneading

Glaze

- 1 egg
- 3 tablespoons milk

Directions

With two spoons or the back of a spoon in a shallow bowl, rub saffron threads and one teaspoon of sugar together and set aside. Heat the milk to lukewarm, baby formula temperature, and add the melted butter along with the saffron-sugar mixture.

Combine the yeast with about ¼ cup of the warm saffron milk in a large bowl. Stir it gently. Sprinkle it with 1 tablespoon of the sugar and ⅛ teaspoon salt. Set it aside to "proof" (basically wake up and start growing) for five minutes. Add the remainder of the sugar, the milk, 3 cups of flour and the beaten egg, and stir briskly with a wooden spoon. You can also use an electric mixer with a dough hook. Sprinkle ¼ cup of flour on top and knead dough in the bowl for several more minutes, adding more flour if the dough is too sticky to handle. The dough should become very stretchy and resilient.

Keeping the dough in the bowl, shape it into a ball. Dust the top with flour; cover with a clean damp cloth and let it rise in a warm, dry place until double in size, about 60 to 90 minutes.

Turn the dough out onto a floured counter or tabletop and knead for 5 to 10 minutes, adding flour as needed to keep the dough from sticking. Try not to add too much flour, as this will make the buns tough and hard (you want them soft). Divide the dough into 24 small pieces and, using your hands, roll the dough first into balls, then into ropes and finally into figure-eight or "S" shapes.

As the buns are formed, place them on a buttered or greased cookie sheet. You can also cover the cookie sheet with a piece of parchment paper. Push raisins into the dough as desired for decoration.

Cover the buns with a clean cloth and let rise again until double in size, about 30 minutes. Preheat oven to 425° F. Make the glaze by beating 1 egg with 3 tablespoons milk. Brush the tops of the buns with the glaze just before baking. Bake 5 to 10 minutes. Watch them closely. When they are evenly brown, take them out of the oven to cool on a rack.

The Christmas Candle

Some families light a large candle symbolizing the Lord on Christmas Eve. This candle burns through the Holy Night. The candle is then lit every night during the Christmas season.

In the Slavic nations, the blessed candle is put on the table for the Christmas feast. • The Ukrainians place their Christmas candle in a loaf of bread—the bread of Life. • In France and England, the candle is often made of three candles twisted together in honor of the Holy Trinity. • In parts of South America, the candle shines through a paper lantern with symbols and pictures of the Nativity on its sides. • In Germany, the candle burns on top of a wooden pole decorated with evergreens. In another version of this tradition small candles are placed on the shelves of a wooden structure shaped like a pyramid, adorned with fir or laurel. • In Ireland, a large candle decorated with holly is lit on Christmas Eve, and the entire family prays for all its dear ones, living and dead. The Irish place candles in the windows and leave the door open for Mary and Joseph on Christmas Eve. • In Labrador, turnips and other vegetables hold lighted candles to celebrate Christ's birth.

Julebrod (Christmas Bread)

Ingredients

- 2 cups scalded milk
- 1 cup butter, melted
- 2 teaspoons salt
- 1 cup white sugar
- 2 tablespoons or packages active dry yeast
- ½ cup warm water
- 8½ cups all-purpose flour
- 1 tablespoon ground cardamom
- ½ cup candied cherries, sliced
- ½ cup chopped candied citron
- 1 cup golden raisins
- 1 egg white, beaten

Directions

Sprinkle the yeast over the water in a small cup and let it dissolve.

Scald the milk and pour it into a large bowl. Add the melted butter or margarine, salt and sugar. When the milk mixture is lukewarm add the yeast and water. Stir in cardamom, cherries, raisins and citron. Stir in 4 cups flour and stir briskly with a wooden spoon. You can also use an electric mixer with a dough hook. The dough should become very stretchy and resilient. Cover, and place in a warm place. Let rise for about 2 hours, or till doubled in bulk. This is called a "sponge".

Punch the sponge down. Work in remaining flour until soft dough forms. Try not to add much more flour than called for, as this will make the bread tough and hard. You want it soft.

Let rise in warm place for 2 to 3 hours, or until doubled.

Knead slightly, and form into 4 round loaves or rounded bun shapes. Place on greased cookie sheets. Let rise for 1 to 2 hours, or till doubled. Brush loaves with beaten egg white.

Bake the loaves at 350° F for 30 to 40 minutes, or until golden brown. Bake the buns at the same temperature for only 10 minutes. Watch them carefully, especially the bottoms, to make sure they don't get too brown. Remove from the oven and cool on wire racks. You can decorate these buns with an icing sugar and orange juice glaze when they're cooled.

Makes 4 loaves.

Who Was Saint Lucy?
The Story of an Early Christian Martyr

Saint Lucy lived about three hundred years after Jesus was born. Her parents were wealthy, and they were Christians, even though many people in the world at that time were still pagans, who worshipped other gods.

Saint Lucy and her family lived in the town of Syracuse in Sicily. Her father died when she was still a baby, and she was raised by her mother, Eutychia, a pious and devoted Christian. She grew up loving Jesus and wanting to give her whole life to Him.

When Lucy was still a young girl, she made a vow that she would remain unmarried and would serve God all her life. She kept this vow a secret, so as not to draw any attention to herself.

When she was older, her mother, who did not know of her vow, promised a rich young man of Syracuse that Lucy would marry him. It was a common thing for parents to arrange their children's marriages, so the young man and Lucy's mother were quite sure that this would be acceptable to Lucy.

But Lucy didn't want to marry at all, and she prayed to God for some way to persuade her mother not to make her marry the young man. She tried several times to persuade her mother that she did not want to marry anyone. She avoided meeting the young man as often as she could. Both her mother and the young man were angry with her, but she kept her secret and didn't tell them of her vow.

Eutychia became ill with a constant hemorrhage, which made her very weak. Lucy reminded her mother of the story in the Gospels of the woman who was cured of a hemorrhage by touching Christ's cloak. She suggested that they make a pilgrimage to the tomb of Saint Agatha to pray for healing.

While at the tomb, Eutychia was miraculously healed. Saint Agatha appeared to Lucy in a dream and told her that she would be martyred for Christ's sake. Lucy told her mother of her vow and how she had prayed for some way to change her mother's mind. Grateful for healing, Eutychia allowed Lucy to keep her vow.

Angered by this change in plans, the young suitor denounced Lucy as a Christian to the governor of the region. Being a Christian had become very dangerous in the year 303 because the Emperor Diocletian's edicts began one of the worst persecutions yet. When Lucy was found guilty, a judge ordered that she be sold into slavery [at a brothel]. That, he thought, would change her mind about being a Christian.

Soldiers came to take her away, but no matter how hard they tried, Lucy stood as if rooted to the ground. The soldiers were frightened by this, a small young woman as unmovable as a mountain. They poured oil on her head and set her on fire to try to make her move, but her body was not burned. They demanded to know why she was not harmed, and she replied that the power of the Lord Jesus Christ protected her. Finally, they stabbed her in the throat with a sword, and she died.

Saint Lucy was welcomed into Heaven by Jesus, whom she had loved so much that she had died for Him. Since that time, many legends have grown up around her. Some say that she was tortured and her eyes were put out before her death. For this reason, Saint Lucy is invoked as the patron of those with eye ailments.

Saint Luke and the Christmas Story

Saint Luke was an evangelist, a poet, a physician and an artist. He is also the narrator of the Holy Infancy of the Savior of Mankind. Saint Luke did not invent the Christmas narrative, but he wrote down many of the details about Jesus' birth. In doing so, he preserved one of the best loved stories in all of history.

Saint Luke was the evangelist who provides us with most of our information and evidence about the conception, infancy and childhood of Jesus. He, along with Matthew, points out how many of the circumstances answer the prophesies. It is widely believed, and certainly possible, that one of the people Luke interviewed, perhaps at greater length than any other witness, was Mary, the mother of Christ, herself.

Luke's descriptions include the Annuciation, the announcement by the Archangel Gabriel that Mary had been chosen to be the mother of Christ. These words of Luke are the basis for the Hail Mary and the *Angelus* (Latin for angel). He also gives the only Gospel account of the Visitation. One of the most beautiful prayers, the *Magnificat*, appears in this passage. In addition, Luke is the only evangelist to describe the presentation of the child Jesus in the Temple according to Jewish custom. These five events that Luke describes—the Annuciation, the Visitation, the Nativity, the Presentation and the Finding of Jesus in the Temple—comprise the joyful mysteries of the Rosary.

Saint Luke never married, and he lived to be 84 years old. According to tradition, he was a skilled artist, and several pictures of Our Blessed Lady are attributed to him. Some accounts claim that his portrait of Our Blessed Lady, since lost, was used as inspiration for the icon of Our Lady of Perpetual Help. His feast day is celebrated on October 18.

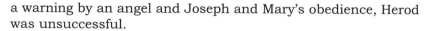

and bear a son, and his name shall be called Emmanuel" (which means, God with us.) When Joseph woke from sleep, he

The Feast of the Holy Innocents

Martyrs
Patron of choirboys
Feast day: December 28

Unlike most of the other feasts and celebrations of the season, the Feast of the Holy Innocents is a solemn, sorrowful occasion. In the story and history of the Church, it is a foreshadowing of the Crucifixion of Christ and the persecution of early Christians. (CCC 530.) Saint Stephen's day (also known as Boxing Day) on December 26 is another solemn occasion, for similar reasons. Saint Stephen was the first Christian martyr.

Told of the birth of the new King of the Jews by the Eastern Magi, and cheated of easy discovery by their not returning to his palace in Jerusalem, Herod ordered the slaughter of all male children under the age of two in the town of Bethlehem. By this brutal but expedient massacre, he sought to eliminate the threat that Christ's birth posed to his throne. Thanks to

a warning by an angel and Joseph and Mary's obedience, Herod was unsuccessful.

The exact chronological order of events surrounding Christ's birth is unclear, and a skeptical early teen will undoubtedly wonder how Mary and Joseph could flee the Massacre of the Holy Infants on December 28, yet present Jesus at the Temple on February 2 (at the Feast of the Presentation, or Candlemas Day). Point out to them and other doubting Thomases that in those days, both news and men traveled slowly. The Holy Family may have stayed in Bethlehem for months after the birth of Jesus, while Mary recovered her health and Jesus grew old enough for a long journey. The Magi probably didn't arrive in Jerusalem for some months after the appearance of the star and Christ's birth. It is entirely possible that the Flight into Egypt took place when Christ was a year or more old. It's for this reason that Herod condemned every male child under two years of age.

The day is traditionally observed as a day of mourning and was considered a highly unpopular day for marriages, indeed, for beginning any enterprise.

In the domestic church, the Feast of the Holy Innocents can be observed as an opportunity to honor and bless children, while at the same time teaching them of the occasional harshness of the world toward people of faith.

Using the same theme of innocence and purity, as suggested for the celebration of the Feast of the Immaculate Conception, serve a white meal. Add the variation of martyrdom with red garnishes, such as tomatoes or ketchup. For dessert, serve white cake or ice cream with strawberry or raspberry sauce.

This is a good time to begin the practice of blessing your children. A special father's blessing (because *you* are the priest of the domestic church, the home, dads) for this day and a nightly blessing of the family before they go to bed are powerful spiritual weapons of protection for your family as they grow, mature and go out into the world.

Blessings and Holy Water

Every home should have a font for holy water by the front door, so that the family members can bless themselves as they enter and leave the house. This continues and reinforces the Epiphany blessing of the lintels, asking for physical, spiritual, emotional and mental protection of all who cross the threshold. (CCC 1668–70.)

Holy water can also be used at evening prayers to bless the children before they head off to bed. The father, in his office as head of the family (as Christ is Head of the Church), should bless his children every day. These special moments express his love and caring protection of them and give them the graces and confidence necessary to face both the challenges and trials of their growing lives.

Holy water is also useful to bless a new house, a new car, the bedroom of the latest child having nightmares, an Advent wreath, the Christmas tree and the Easter feast, and may be used for other family celebrations and devotions.

Blessed holy water is available at your church. Some churches have special dispensers with taps for holy water at the back of the church. In other parishes, you may have to ask the priest or sacristan for holy water. Bring a small bottle with you.

A useful little item is a "holy water sprinkler". Any member of the family old enough to handle a pocket knife can make one. The most important thing to remember when using a knife is to cut away from yourself. Never point or push the knife blade toward your hand or body!

All you need is a 15-cm (6-inch) stick from a tree or bush outside and your pocket knife.

- Carefully peel the bark off the stick.
- Carve one end of the stick to a neat blunt point, just so that it is not raggedy.
- Split the other end of the stick in half by standing the stick up on a surface and gently pushing the knife blade down-

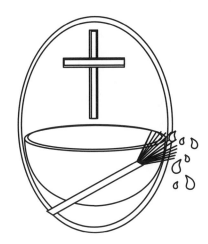

ward into it. Keep both hands on the back of the blade and use the pressure of the knife to keep the stick upright.

- Alternatively, you can lay the stick down on a cutting board or piece of wood outside (not on Mom's counter or dining room table!), and slice into the end of the stick. If you are right-handed, hold the stick in your left hand with the end you want to cut pointing to the right. If you are left-handed, hold the stick with your right hand with the end you want to cut pointing to the left.
- Split about 1 cm (½ inch) into the stick. Split it again into quarters, then eights, then sixteenths, until the end of the stick is like frayed rope.

And it's done!

Make several and give them away to all your friends and relatives. Keep one with each font and bottle of holy water (recycled spice bottles are perfect for holy water). The holy water sprinkler is used by dipping it into the holy water and flicking the drops off its end, just as the priest does at Mass.

Saint Stephen's Day

December 26, the day after Christmas, is the feast of Saint Stephen. One of the first deacons, he was also the first Christian martyr (see Acts 6 and 7 for an account). In some countries December 26 is a traditional day for giving gifts to tradespeople or to the needy. In England it is called Boxing Day.

The Feast of Saint Stephen is mentioned in the hymn "Good King Wenceslaus". Also a Christian martyr, Saint Wenceslaus was born in 907 A.D. near Prague. He was educated as a Christian. When he became king, he tried to rule with justice and mercy, but he encountered opposition. His own brother attacked him while he was on the way to Mass. After a struggle, friends of his brother killed Wenceslaus. Like Saint Stephen, who prayed for those who stoned him, Saint Wenceslaus died asking God's forgiveness for his brother. (The feast of Saint Wenceslaus is celebrated on September 28.)

Good King Wenceslaus

Good King Wenceslaus looked out
  On the Feast of Stephen,
When the snow lay round about,
  Deep, and crisp, and even.
Brightly shone the moon that night,
  Tho' the frost was cruel,
When a poor man came in sight,
  Gathering winter fuel.

"Hither, page, and stand by me,
  If thou know'st it, telling,
Yonder peasant, who is he?
  Where and what his dwelling?"
"Sire, he lives a good league hence,
  Underneath the mountain,
Right against the forest fence,
  By Saint Agnes' fountain."

"Bring me flesh, and bring me wine,
  Bring me pine logs hither:
Thou and I will see him dine
  When we bear them thither."
Page and monarch forth they went,
  Forth they went together,
Through the rude wind's wild lament
  And the bitter weather.

"Sire, the night is darker now,
  And the wind blows stronger;
Fails my heart I know not how,
  I can go no longer."
"Mark my footsteps, my good page,
  Tread thou in them boldly:
Thou shalt find the winter's rage
  Freeze thy blood less coldly."

In his master's steps he trod,
  Where the snow lay dinted;
Heat was in the very sod
  Which the Saint had printed.
Therefore, Christian men, be sure,
  Wealth or rank possessing,
Ye who now will bless the poor,
  Shall yourselves find blessing.

Crafts

Christmas Cross-Stitch Patterns

Several years ago, we began to restore Advent in our home. In addition to following the Jesse Tree readings and lighting an Advent wreath every evening, we got rid of any decoration that had a secular Christmas theme. Out went Santa!

This left a bit of a problem, though. It is difficult to find liturgically appropriate decorations and designs for the Advent and Christmas season. Snowmen, candy canes, elves and stockings abound, but shepherds, stars, birds, wheat sheaves and mangers seem to be in short supply. So, over the years I have created my own decorations, including cross-stitch patterns.

The following designs are small and simple cross-stitch patterns suitable for Christmas tree ornaments (which is how I have used them) or to be embroidered onto bookmarks, place mats and napkins. They are small and simple enough that mid-aged children, eight and up, should be able to finish them quickly.

A Short Course in Cross-Stitch

Bringing the thread through at the lower right-hand side, insert the needle 1 block up and 1 block to the left and bring out 1 block down, thus forming a half cross; continue in this way to the end of the row. Complete the upper half of the cross as shown.

Cross-stitch may be worked either from right to left or left to right, but it is important that the upper stroke of all crosses should lie in the same direction.

(For all crafts and other artistic efforts, see CCC 2501.)

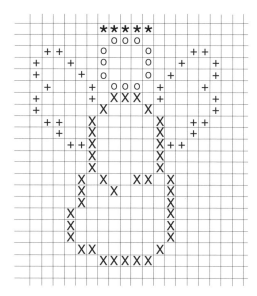

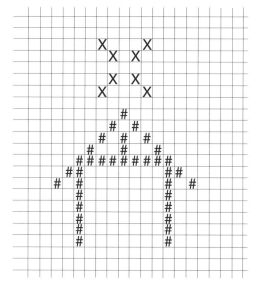

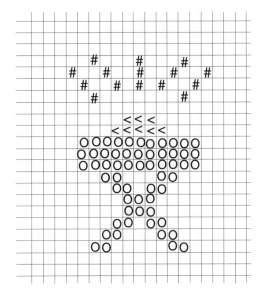

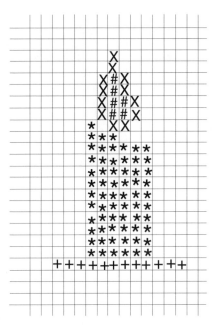

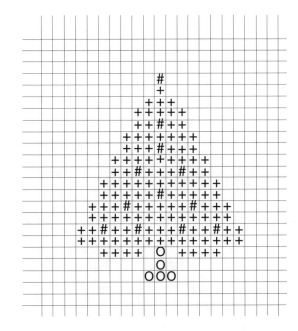

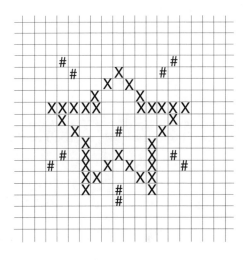

Making Gift Boxes

This is a great Christmas craft activity for boys and girls aged eight and up. Our boys spent weeks experimenting with different styles of paper and making tinier and tinier boxes that fit inside each other.

Using the pattern given here, you can make boxes of any size, out of almost any material. Old Christmas cards or calendar pictures make great boxes. You can use these boxes as gift wrapping, give them as gifts, or use them yourself to store small Lego, Meccano, or model pieces.

Tools and Materials

- a pencil
- a ruler
- some clear tape
- some old Christmas cards or other heavy paper

Directions

First decide what you want to show on the outside of your box. Draw a light pencil rectangle around it. Press hard at the corners, so that the dots show through on the back side.

On the back of the paper, draw diagonal lines (X) connecting the corners.

After that, draw the fold lines, connecting the corner dots in a rectangle. Make sure that the fold lines meet exactly on the diagonal lines you drew.

Next, draw the cutting lines. The sides should be at least an inch outside the fold lines, the ends an inch and a quarter.

Cut out the box along the cut lines.

Fold along the fold lines. Use the edge of a ruler to keep them straight. Fold the sides of the box up first and the cut ends in. Tape them together.

Then fold the ends of the box up and fold them over the sides. Tape the ends on the inside of the box.

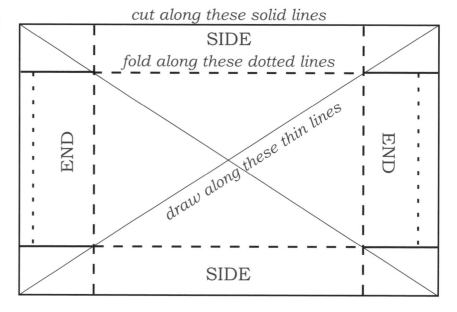

cut along these solid lines

SIDE

fold along these dotted lines

END

draw along these thin lines

END

SIDE

To make a lid for your box, cut another rectangle the same size, but make the fold lines ⅜ of an inch farther apart (closer to the outside edges of the rectangle).

This will make the lid just big enough to fit over the top of your box.

Experiment with different sizes of rectangle and fold lines to make deeper, shallower, bigger or smaller boxes.

Big Boxes and Little Boxes

How tiny a box can you make?

How many boxes can you nest one inside the other?

Perfect Playdough

It's important for children to feel that they are making a contribution to the family Christmas. At the same time, it's hard to come up with crafts that satisfy both their creative urges and their short attention span, have good enough results with a child's abilities and don't make so much mess that they are more trouble than they are worth. Seriously, it isn't worth having a special craft-moment with the kids if you're going to be cleaning it up for three precious hours you can't spare afterward. Paint on the living room furniture is not my idea of a great decorating feature!

So, if your tree looks a little bare, your five year old wants to give Grandma a present at the last minute, or you just need something simple but fairly tidy to keep the children occupied while you clean the bathroom or peel potatoes, this great craft for all ages is something you might want to try.

This is the best baker's dough I've ever found. It stays white while baking, it doesn't curl, and hanging holes don't shrink shut. It handles and cuts well, and it takes paint perfectly because it doesn't have lots of grainy salt in it. It makes great decorations for the tree, and picture frames, and lots of other items.

Ingredients

- 2 cups baking soda
- 1 cup flour
- ¼ cup cold water

Directions

Mix the three ingredients in a saucepan.

Cook gently over medium heat, stirring often until it is the consistency of moist mashed potatoes. Don't let it get too dry.

Put it out onto a plate and allow to cool. Don't let the kids touch it at this point, even though it looks ready. It's very hot!

Instead, cover it with a damp cloth and allow to cool to handling temperature.

Turn out onto counter and knead until smooth.

Roll out to approximately ¼ inch thick and cut as desired. Remember to cut hanging holes now, if you're making tree decorations.

Bake at 325° F. Bake the shapes until they are firm or hard to the touch and just barely beginning to brown on the underside. The shapes should stay white.

Cool in the oven. This is important—slow cooling avoids cracking.

Decorate as desired, finishing with a coat of varnish, acrylic, nail polish, or white glue mixed with a little water. The point is to waterproof it so that moisture in the air doesn't make it go soft and "gicky".

Table-Top Angel

This angel takes a few hours and some skill to create, but it is still quite easy and also quite beautiful. There are lots of opportunities to make this angel special. The fabric for the body and skirt, the material to make the wings and the way you paint the face will all give your angel an individual and unique appearance.

Tools

- glue
- stapler
- needle and thread
- embroidery thread and embroidery needle
- pins, scissors
- ruler
- clothespins

Materials

Start by assembling the materials you need for the:

Head

- Styrofoam ball, about 1½ inch in diameter. You can use a ball of polyester filling, or a large bead, or a piece of modeling clay or playdough, just about anything as long as it is round and the right size.
- circle about 6 inches in diameter of white or skin-colored fabric

Hair

- yarn, spanish moss, a gold pot-scrubber, sheep's wool

Body

- light cardboard, such as a cereal box
- at least 42 inches of 6- to 8-inch wide lace or cotton embroidered edging (the edge of an old embroidered tablecloth looks really nice). One layer will do if the fabric is closely woven. If the fabric is really lacy you will want two or three times as much fabric cut to 36-inch lengths.

Arms

- white pipe cleaner
- strip of fabric used for head, about 2 inches wide and 10 inches long

Wings

- 18 inches of 3-inch-wide wire-edged ribbon, or more of the lace fabric used for the body, or a paper doily

Decoration

- narrow ribbon
- small beads
- paint or marker for face
- small folded paper for a book, a small gold horn, anything else an angel might hold

Directions

Making the Head

Cut out the circle of fabric for the head and drape it over the ball. Gather it together at the bottom and tie a piece of thread around the gathered fabric. Smooth the fabric on one side of the ball for the face.

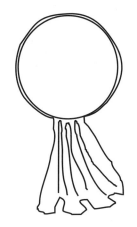

Making the Body

Cut out the body from the light cardboard using the diagram as a guide. Experiment to get the size you want. Bring the circle together to make a cone, and glue, staple or tape it securely. Make sure the hole at the top is big enough for the "neck" of the angel's head.

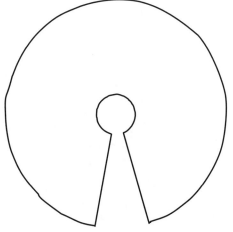

Insert the angel's neck into the hole and tape, staple or sew it in place (poke the needle through the cardboard and then through the neck fabric). Do it firmly enough that the head stays upright.

Then, take a 36-inch skirt fabric piece and hem along the plain (unembroidered) edge and down both sides. Run long basting stitches along the top edge and pull them to gather the fabric.

Put the gathered edge around the neck of the angel, and gather it some more until it fits well. Tie these gathering threads together.

With a needle and thread sew a stitch at the back of the neck into the skirt fabric; wrap the thread around the angel's neck a few times and take another stitch. Stitch into the neck fabric too, making sure that the skirt is firmly gathered and attached and that the head is straight.

If you are using more than one layer of skirt, repeat the steps.

Judea in place of his father Herod, he was afraid to go there, and being warned in a dream he withdrew to the district of Galilee. And he went and dwelt in a city called

Making the Arms

If you want the arms together at the front of the doll, follow the directions on the illustrations. Thread the clasped hands and arms through the sleeve piece and sew the ends of the arms together, making a circle.

Then pull the arms around until the sewn seam is inside the middle of the sleeve. Put the sleeve arm assembly over the angel's head and fasten it at the back of the neck with a few stitches.

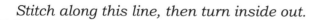

Stitch along this line, then turn inside out.

Tie a knot to look like hands.

If you want separated hands, sew the arm piece together and cut it in half. Sew across one cut end of each arm piece. Turn the arm pieces right side out, and push a folded pipe cleaner inside each one. Staple or sew the pipe cleaner to the open end of the arm piece.

Now, thread the arms into the sleeves, making the two open ends meet in the middle of the sleeve piece. Fasten them in place with a few stitches. Sew the sleeve arm assembly onto the back of the angel's neck and bend the arms to the angle you like.

Making the Sleeves

Cut the sleeve piece out of the remaining skirt fabric. Fold it, right sides together, and sew it.

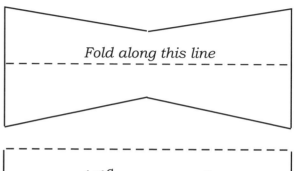

Fold along this line

Stitch along *this line*

Making the Wings

If you are using a piece of skirt fabric for the wings, cut it lengthwise so that it is only 3 or 4 inches wide. Gather an 8-inch length tightly with long stitches and wrapping stitches, then fasten it to the angel's back, on top of the sleeves. Repeat for the other wing.

If you are using a circular doily or piece of lace, bunch the fabric together in the middle as shown in the illustration below.

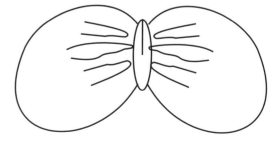

If you are using wire-edged or plain ribbon, tie a big bow in the ribbon and fasten it to the sleeve at the back of the angel.

Finishing the Angel

Put hair on the angel. Depending on what you are using, sew or glue the hair in place.

Put a face on the angel. Simple black circles for eyes and an oval for a singing mouth is enough. For a closed mouth use a slightly curved red or black line. It is important to remember that eyes are halfway down a head. The hair takes up a lot of head. Try lightly marking the eyes and mouth with a pencil or pins stuck into the head, until you are satisfied with the look of the angel.

To decorate the angel, try a long piece of bright narrow ribbon tied around the neck and hanging down the front of the angel's skirt. Add a halo of seed beads or narrow ribbon around the head and something in the angel's hands. If the back of the angel looks a bit messy because of all the pieces and sewing, glue a piece of ribbon or fabric over it all, down the middle of the wings to hide the rough edges.

Admire Your Handiwork

Now, put the angel on the table in front of you; arrange the skirt smoothly, make the wings straight, get the arms at exactly the right angle. Doesn't it look nice?

Adeste, Fideles

Adéste, fidéles, laeti, triumphántes,
Venite, venite in Béthlehem.
Natum vidéte, Regem angelórum,
  Veníte adorémus, veníte adorémus,
  Veníte adorémus Dóminum.

Deum de Deo, Lumen de Lúmine,
Gestant puellae víscera.
Deum verum, génitum, non factum.
  Veníte adorémus, veníte adorémus,
  Veníte adorémus Dóminum.

Cantet nunc Io, chorus angelórum,
Cantet nunc aula caeléstium.
Glória, glória in excélsis Deo.
  Veníte adorémus, veníte adorémus,
  Veníte adorémus Dóminum.

Ergo qui natus die hodiérna,
Jesu, tibi sit glória.
Patris aetérnae Verbum caro factum.
  Veníte adorémus, veníte adorémus,
  Veníte adorémus Dóminum.

Easy Angels for the Tree

These are easy Christmas tree decorations, to sew and hang on your tree. Each can be made to look a little different by changing the fabric and the angle of the wings, feet and head.

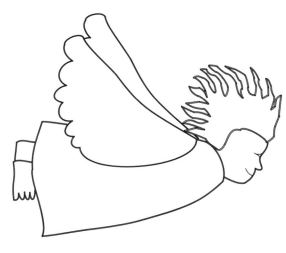

These angels take well to a variety of construction methods. They can be sewn together by hand or by machine, with a simple running stitch (up and down), a "whip" stitch (over and over the edge) or a blanket stitch (interlocking "L" shapes over the edge). The angels can also be glued together with white glue.

Getting Started

This pattern is simple enough that a four to eight year old can make one with help, an eight to ten year old with supervision and older than that, by themselves. In addition, they're simple enough that they go together quickly and are satisfying for small children who want to see results NOW!

Trace or photocopy and cut out the pattern pieces shown on the next page. If you want, you can make them larger or smaller.

Help your children collect the material, or let them be creative and see what they come up with. You'll need:

*   some fabric scraps:
    *   a nice color for the angel's dress
    *   white or gold or lacy for the wings
    *   a skin color for her head and feet

*   yellow or brown for her hair (if you want, the angel's hair can be strands of yarn sewn or glued on instead of fabric)
*   sewing pins
*   embroidery thread and needles
*   white glue, markers

Cut out the fabric according to the directions on the pattern pieces.

Making the Angel

First, pin the head and feet pieces between the two body pieces at an angle that you like. Sew or glue the body pieces together, making sure that you catch the feet and head in your stitching.

Next, pin the wing pieces onto the body piece, one wing piece on each side. If you have cut out four wing pieces, because your fabric is a bit thin or floppy, put two wings together to make one wing piece and sew them together first, then attach it to the body.

Do the same with the other pair of wing pieces.

Then put hair on your angel. You can pin the hair pieces on either side of the head and sew them on the same way you have sewn on the wings, or you can attach strands of yarn or embroidery cotton along the top edge of the angel's head and let it hang down.

Finishing Up

Finally, take a piece of yarn or embroidery cotton about 8 inches long and thread it on a needle.

Between the wings, near the angel's "shoulders", push the needle through the angel's body and draw half the thread through. Pull the needle off the thread and tie the two ends of thread together into a strong knot. The angel will fly level, soar upward or look downward, depending on where you put your needle through for the hanging string.

Hang up your angel and make another one!

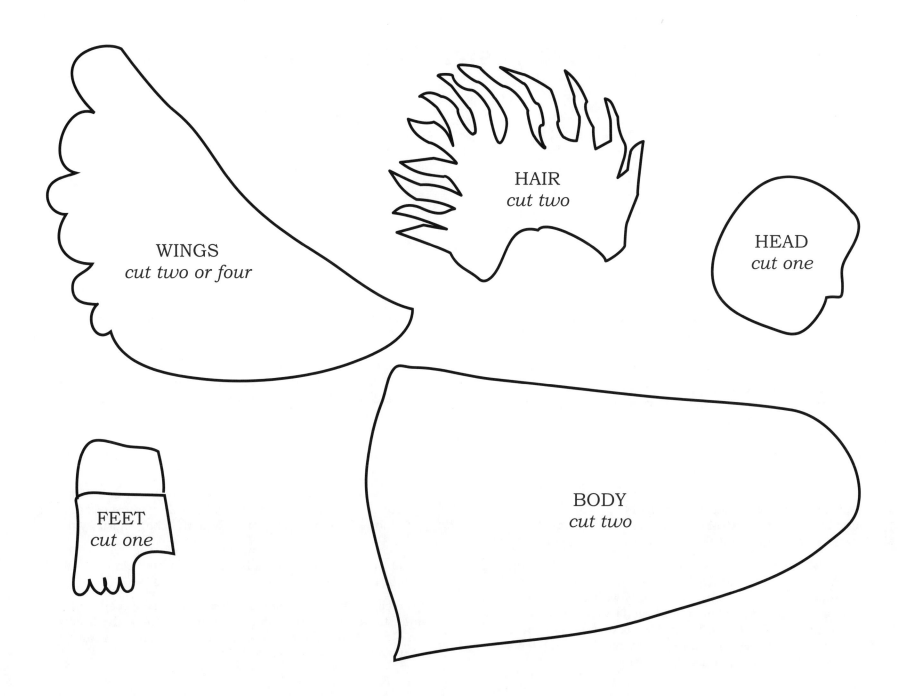

WINGS
cut two or four

HAIR
cut two

HEAD
cut one

FEET
cut one

BODY
cut two

Wheat Design Table Runner

Wheat plays a strong role in many countries' Catholic traditions. It is the main ingredient in many kinds of bread, the staple food for countless diets. The connection to the "Bread of Life" is inescapable. For this alone, wheat is powerfully symbolic.

But there's more. Wheat is ground and sifted to make flour and bread. Many separate grains combine to make one substance. We are tested and "sifted" in life, and many separate souls combine in the Church, the Mystical Body of Christ. The finest flour is used in the making of hosts—even more symbolism. It's not surprising, then, that special bread and other wheat dishes are traditional at the major feasts of several countries.

In addition, many stories have arisen to explain, expand or embellish wheat's central importance. Here's a tale from the Russian tradition about the miraculous growth of a wheat field:

> As the Holy Family hurried away from Bethlehem after the angel's warning that the Infant was in danger, they passed a farmer in his fields outside the city walls. It was early in the morning, just after dawn, and the farmer was sowing grain in his freshly plowed fields. He nodded as they passed. Joseph, leading the donkey carrying Mary and Jesus, smiled and raised a hand in greeting.

Later that day, almost at evening time, a group of Roman soldiers came marching out of Bethlehem on the same road. All that day, Bethlehem had echoed with screams, sobs and the sounds of running feet. The farmer had wondered at the sounds, but had continued working, not wanting to bring himself and his family to the Roman authorities' notice by investigating. Better to stay silent, hidden and safe, he thought.

The Roman soldiers called the farmer out of his field and harshly demanded, "Have a man and woman carrying a baby passed this way?"

"Oh, yes", the farmer assured them, trembling. Fleetingly, he felt sorry for the couple. They had little chance of escaping the long arm of Roman punishment. What had they done?

"They passed as I was sowing my grain", he continued. And half turning, he waved a hand toward his field, now filled with tall grain, ripe and ready to harvest.

In Ukrainian tradition, hay or wheat straw is spread on the dinner table, under the table cloth, to symbolize the Infant Jesus' first bed. This table runner follows that tradition (sort of), but it's a good deal easier and tidier.

To make the runner, you will need:

- unbleached or white canvas
- acrylic craft paint (I suggest white, black and gold, though other colors could be used)
- fine paintbrushes
- carbon paper and a ballpoint pen
- paper clips

First, cut the canvas to the size you want, to fit your table. It should be about twelve to eighteen inches wide and as long as you'd like. Iron it with a steam iron set on high to get it absolutely wrinkle-free.

Paint the canvas with two or three coats of white acrylic craft paint. Work the paint into the weave of the canvas with the brush. It helps to thin the first coat of paint with water, then when it has dried, to use unthinned paint for the next coats. Let the canvas dry.

Next, place the carbon paper and wheat pattern on the painted canvas, holding them in place with paper clips. If you want the pattern a different size, have it enlarged with a photocopier. Trace the wheat pattern onto the canvas. Carefully remove the pattern and carbon paper. If you want, go over the lines on the canvas with a sharp pencil.

Begin painting the pattern onto the table runner, outlining each shape first, then after the outline has dried, filling in the shapes. Some parts look best simply outlined, some look good filled in. Decide as you go along.

When the painting is finished, allow the runner to dry well before using. Acrylic paint is water resistant once dry, so the runner will stand up to moderate use and wiping with a damp cloth. Store it rolled in a cylinder.

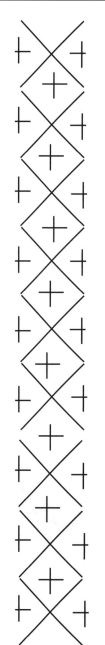

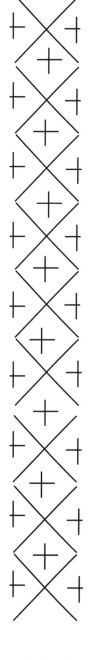

Another Idea

This carbon paper tracing method will work to paint any of the coloring patterns in this book onto canvas. How about a set of Nativity place mats?

Alternatively, you could trace the wheat pattern onto unpainted embroidery canvas and embroider the pattern for a tablecloth, pillow or banner. Use running-stitch or chain stitch for outlining, french knots for grains of wheat, and satin stitch to fill in spaces.

Following the illustration at the beginning of this article, use the wheat pattern on the next page in the center of your runner and these two border patterns on either end.

Enlarge them as necessary with pencil and paper or a photocopier.

Advent, Christmas and Epiphany in the Domestic Church: Crafts

Saints' Symbols

A terrific thing to do with Perfect Playdough or cross-stitch is to make representations of saints' symbols. These symbols can then be hung as Christmas tree decorations and used in name-day celebrations or as year-round decorations honoring a special saint. One year, I made saints' symbols for each of the children from modeling clay. For Andrew, I created a tiny fish, painted it brightly, then enclosed it in a "fishing net" made of a scrap of onion bag. "Come follow me and I will make you fishers of men." It was a great success. For Matthew, I made a little book for his Gospel, Sarah Anne a door, Jonathon James a cockle shell, Faustina a crown and Robert a book. For my husband and me, I made Peter a gold key, and for Catherine a ring.

Some of the saints' symbols graphically demonstrate the method of their martyrdom. Little boys, especially, delight in the "gross" ones. Fortunately no one in our family is named Lawrence or Denis. Here are the symbols for some common names.

Andrew: transverse cross, fish

Anne, grandmother of Jesus: door

Anthony of Padua: Infant Jesus, bread, book, lily

Barbara: tower, ciborium

Bartholomew: knife

Benedict: broken cup, raven, bell

Bernard of Clairvaux: pen, bees

Bridget of Sweden: book, pilgrim's staff

Catherine: broken wheel

Catherine of Ricci: ring, crown, crucifix

Catherine of Siena: cross, ring, lily

Cecilia: organ

Charles Borromeo: communion

Clare of Assisi: monstrance

Denis: head in hands

Dominic: rosary, star

Elizabeth of Hungary: alms, flowers, bread, pitcher

Francis of Assisi: wolf, birds, fish

Francis Xavier: crucifix, bell, vessel

Genevieve: bread, keys, herd, cattle

George: dragon

Gregory I, the Great: tiara, crosier, dove

Helena: cross

James the Greater: pilgrim's staff, shell, key, sword

James the Less: square rule, halberd, club, cockleshell

Jerome: lion

John Berchmans: cross, rosary

John Chrysostom: bees, dove, pen

John of God: alms, a heart, crown of thorns

John the Baptist: lamb, head on a platter, animal skin

John the Evangelist: eagle, chalice, kettle, armor

Joseph, husband of Mary: lily, rod, plane, carpenter's square

Jude: a sword, square rule, club

Justin Martyr: ax, sword

Lawrence: cross, book of the Gospels, gridiron

Louis IX of France: crown of thorns, nails

Lucy: cord, eyes on a dish

Luke: ox, book, brush, palette

Margaret: dragon in chains

Mark: lion, book

Martha: holy water sprinkler, dragon

Matilda: purse, alms

Matthew: winged man, purse, lance

Maurus: scales, spade, crutch

Michael: scales, banner, sword, dragon

Monica: girdle, tears

Nicholas: three purses or balls, anchor, boat

Patrick: cross, harp, serpent, baptismal font, shamrock

Paul: sword, book or scroll

Peter: keys, boat, cock

Philip the Apostle: column

Rita of Cascia: rose, crucifix, thorn

Rock: angel, dog, bread

Rose of Lima: crown of thorns, anchor, city

Sebastian: arrows, crown

Teresa of Avila: heart, arrow, book

Thérèse of Lisieux: roses entwining a crucifix

Thomas Aquinas: chalice, monstrance, dove, ox

Thomas the Apostle: lance, ax

Vincent de Paul: children

Vincent Ferrer: pulpit, cardinal's hat, trumpet

The Holy Helpers

In the fourteenth century when the Black Plague and other epidemics caused death throughout Europe, these "Fourteen Auxiliary Saints" or Holy Helpers were popular. In the panic, death of family and church personnel and general chaos, many people died without receiving the final sacraments. In fear, the living sought the intercession of saints known individually for helping with different symptoms of the plague. They are:

Saint George (April 23) Soldier and martyr. Represented by a dragon. Invoked against the devil.

Saint Blaise (February 3) Bishop. Represented by two candles crossed. Invoked against diseases of the throat.

Saint Erasmus (June 2) Martyr and bishop. Represented by entrails wound around a windlass. Invoked against diseases of the stomach, cramps and colic.

Saint Pantaleon (July 27) Martyr. Represented by nailed hands. Invoked against consumption.

Saint Vitus (June 15) Martyr. Represented by a cross. Invoked against chorea, the bite of poisonous animals.

Saint Christopher (July 25) Represented by Christ on his shoulder. Invoked against storms and accidents in travel.

Saint Denis (October 9) Represented by his head in his hands. Invoked against possession by the devil.

Saint Cyriacus (August 8) Martyr. Represented by deacon's vestments. Invoked against diseases of the eye.

Saint Agathus (May 8) Martyr. Represented by a crown of thorns. Invoked against headache.

Saint Eustachius (September 20) Martyr. Represented by hunting clothes and a stag. Invoked against fire, both temporal and eternal.

Saint Giles (September 1) Hermit. Represented by his Benedictine habit and a hind. Invoked against panic, epilepsy, madness and nightmares.

Saint Margaret (July 20) Martyr. Represented by a dragon in chains. Invoked against pains in the loins, hazardous childbirth.

Saint Barbara (December 4) Martyr. Represented by a tower and the ciborium. Invoked against sudden death.

Saint Catherine (November 25) Martyr. Represented by a broken wheel. Invoked by students, philosophers and speakers.

Saint Michael the Archangel Cross-Stitch Pattern

This famous, and highly effective, prayer is a part of our evening prayers. I created this simple cross-stitch sampler for my children to work. It would make a wonderful Christmas present from the children to Grandma, or from one family to another.

The prayer is 139 stitches wide by 165 stitches high. In 18-count Aida cloth (which has 18 little squares to the inch) the finished piece will measure 7¾ inches by 9⅛ inches. In 12-count Aida cloth, it will measure just over 11½ inches by 13¾ inches.

Some extra cloth on all sides will be needed to frame the prayer, so purchase cloth a few inches larger all around than the dimensions quoted here.

Use whatever colors of thread you'd like, to coordinate with your own decor. Two shades for the border will enhance the twisted appearance. Most of the letters are to be worked in running-stitch or backstitch, and the border and some words are worked in cross-stitch. See page 56 for basic instructions on how to

form a cross-stitch. (Note that overlap in the following patterns is intentional to aid placement.)

A Short Course in Running-Stitch

Running-stitch and backstitch are the same basic stitch, the difference is which side of the fabric you're looking at. Backstitch looks thicker and fuller than running-stitch.

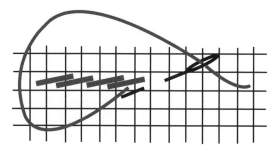

Both are a "two steps forward and one step back" kind of stitch. After coming through the fabric, run the needle across two blocks, then down. Bring the needle back one block and bring it up through the fabric again. Run it two blocks, then down, and so on.

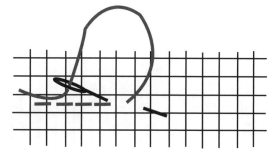

Another Idea

Any one of the coloring pictures would work well as a backstitch or running-stitch embroidery project. Use a single color, such as blue or black, or a range of colors to make the picture.

Saint Michael the Archangel

defend us in this day of battle

Be our protection against

the wickedness and snares of the Devil

May God rebuke him we humbly pray

and do thou O Prince of the Heavenly hosts

cast into hell Satan and all the evil spirits

who prowl the earth seeking the ruin of souls

Advent, Christmas and Epiphany in the Domestic Church: Crafts

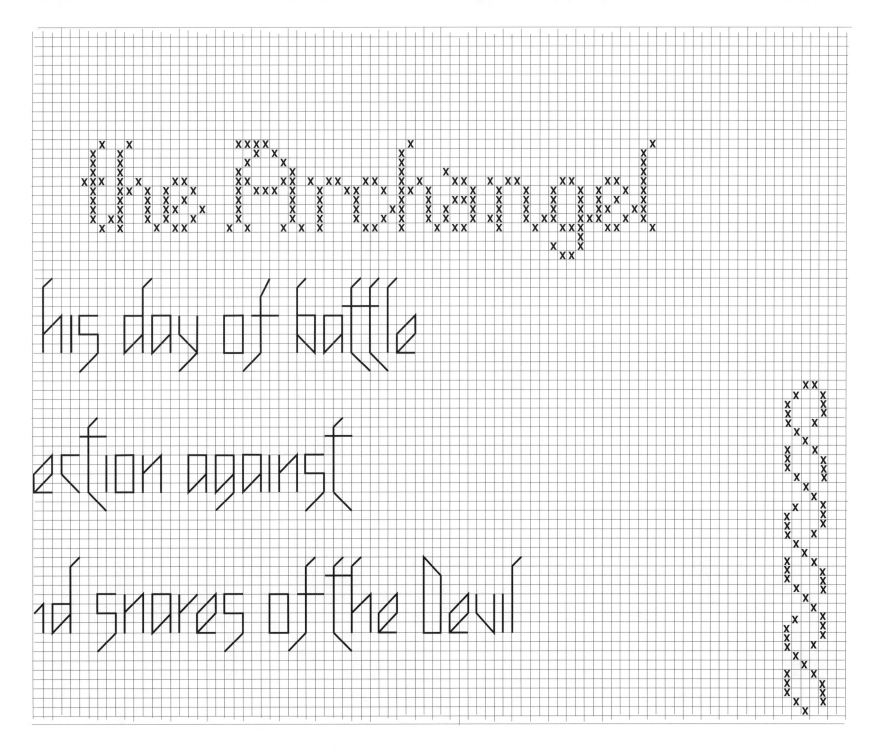

May God rebuke him and do thou O Prince of cast into hell Satan and o who prowl the earth seeki

him we humbly pray

of the Heavenly hosts

and all the evil spirits

eeking the ruin of souls

flesh nor of the will of man, but of God. And the Word became flesh and dwelt among us, full of grace and truth;

Family Photo Stars

This craft is another way to keep the family in the center of the Christmas celebrations with small ornaments made of cardboard and yarn holding photographs of family members. They can be updated yearly, or the collection can be expanded yearly with the latest photograph of each person in the family.

Materials

- Embroidery cotton and 3-strand crewel yarn (yarn is easier to work with, but cotton has brighter colors)
- Cardboard, 1/16 inch to 1/8 inch thick
- Gold foil paper or tinfoil
- White glue and clear tape
- Small passport-photo-sized snapshot of family member
- Craft or dressmakers pins, at least 1/2 inch long
- Ruler and pencil
- Scissors and a utility knife

Directions

Using a utility knife to keep a clean edge, cut two 2-inch squares of cardboard for each ornament. Glue a 2½-inch square of foil to one side of each cardboard square, wrapping the excess smoothly over the edge. Glue another 2-inch square of foil onto the other side of the cardboard, covering the edges of the first piece. Glue both squares together to form an 8-pointed star. Stick a pin in each point, leaving at least 1/16 inch extended.

You're ready to start winding. The thread is wound around the star in a sequence. Keep threads taut and close together. The ornaments will revolve after they are hung, so be sure that the back pattern is also correct.

Before starting a new color, check that the line count of previous color is the same on all sides. Then tie the starting end of the new color to the end of the last color and tuck the knot under the wound threads. Resume winding.

Winding Pattern

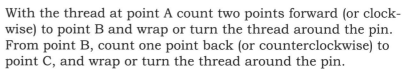

The thread is started from the front, wound around a point, passed to the back to the next point, then continues to alternate front and back.

Tape the end of your first color in the center of the star. It will be hidden later by the photo. Run the thread to point A, and wrap or turn the thread around the pin.

With the thread at point A count two points forward (or clockwise) to point B and wrap or turn the thread around the pin. From point B, count one point back (or counterclockwise) to point C, and wrap or turn the thread around the pin.

Continue this way counting two points forward, one point back, two points forward, one point back, all the way around the star.

Finishing Up

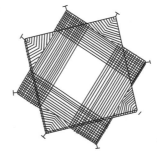

Stop winding when you're pleased with the way it looks, and you have a space left in the center of the star for the photo. Weave the end under the threads at one corner, and knot close to the work. Push the pins all the way into the cardboard now.

To make a hanging loop, cut an 8-inch length of the last color of yarn or cotton. Fold in half. Pull the folded end through the threads and a point or joint. Knot the cut ends and conceal the knot under the threads.

Now, tuck the photo under the threads in the center of the star, making sure that it is secure and centered. If you like, you can put a second photo on the other side of the star.

Coloring Pages

Advent, Christmas and Epiphany in the Domestic Church: Coloring Pages

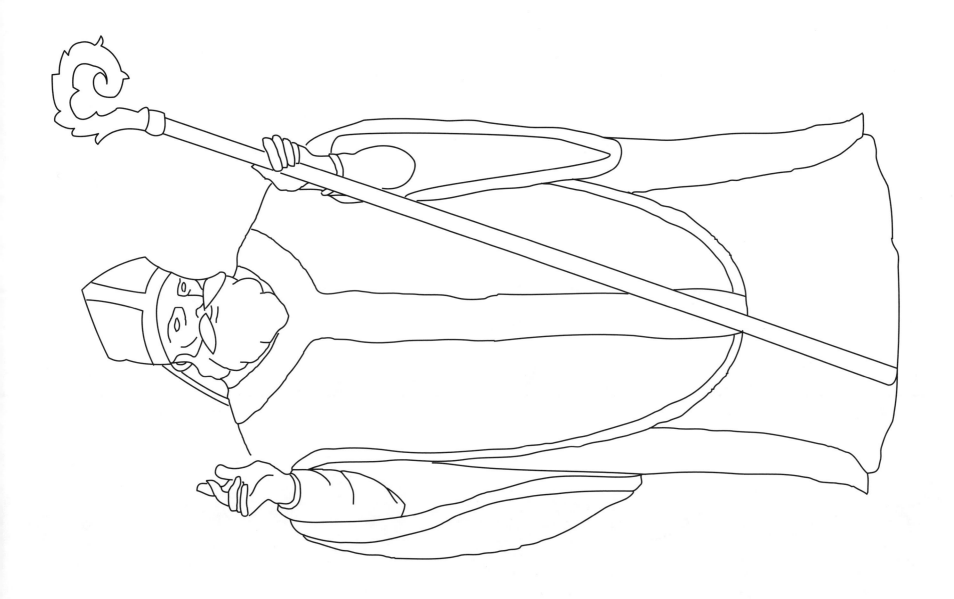

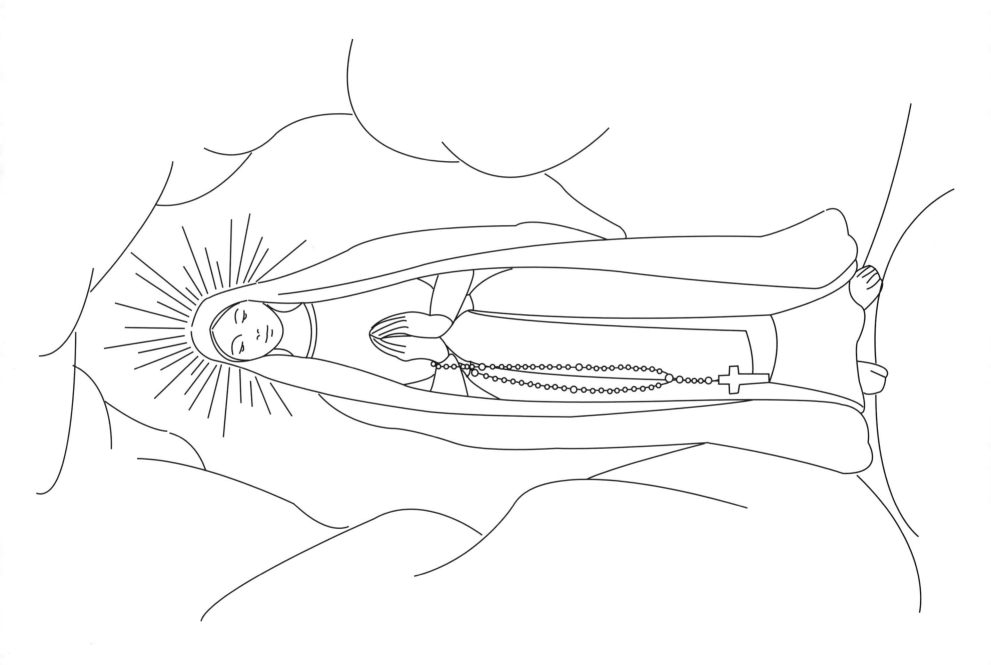

Advent, Christmas and Epiphany in the Domestic Church: Coloring Pages

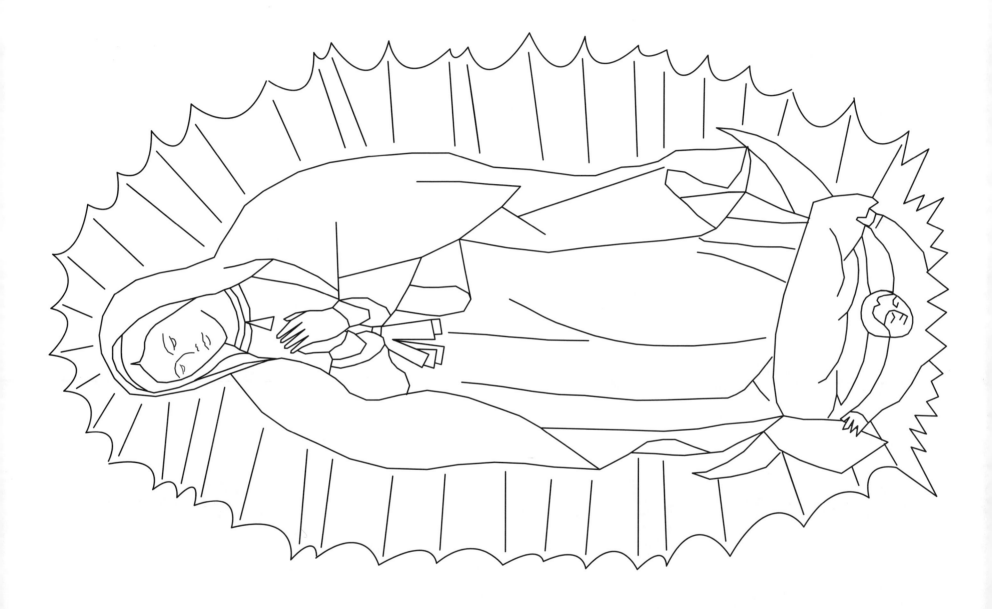

Advent, Christmas and Epiphany in the Domestic Church: Coloring Pages

Advent, Christmas and Epiphany in the Domestic Church: Coloring Pages

Advent, Christmas and Epiphany in the Domestic Church: Coloring Pages

Advent, Christmas and Epiphany in the Domestic Church: Coloring Pages

Advent, Christmas and Epiphany in the Domestic Church: Coloring Pages

Advent, Christmas and Epiphany in the Domestic Church: Coloring Pages

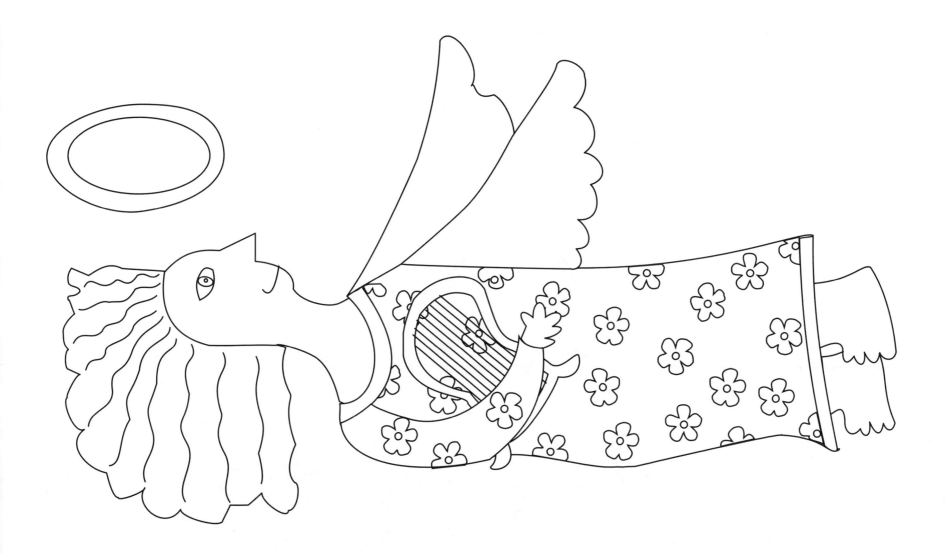

Advent, Christmas and Epiphany in the Domestic Church: Coloring Pages

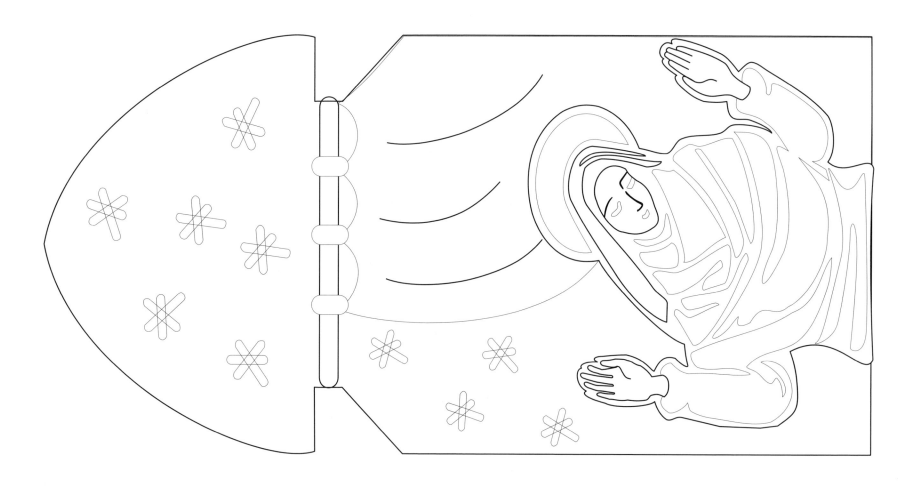

Advent, Christmas and Epiphany in the Domestic Church: Coloring Pages

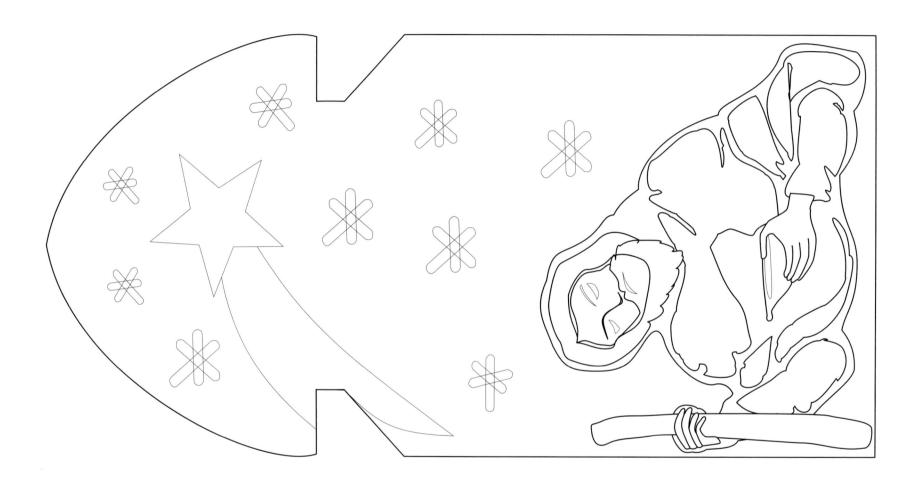

Advent, Christmas and Epiphany in the Domestic Church: Coloring Pages

Subject Index

Additional copies of all coloring pictures and patterns for your personal use are available at: http://www.domestic-church.com/index.dir/index_refills.htm